D1520618

A HISTORY OF SPORTS

IN

NORTH CAROLINA

A History of Sports

in

North Carolina

Jim L. Sumner

Raleigh

Division of Archives and History
North Carolina Department of Cultural Resources

1990

For Ann Sumner

CONTENTS

ILLUSTRATIONS

FOREWORD

North Carolina has always had a rich sports heritage. While most North Carolinians may be familiar with the twentieth-century roots of Atlantic Coast Conference basketball, the bootlegging origins of stock-car racing, and the introduction of golf to the Pinehurst area, they may be less acquainted with the development of quarter horses for racing in the eighteenth century or the baseball games that Union prisoners played at Salisbury during the Civil War.

In a sprightly history of North Carolina's sporting past, Jim L. Sumner combines the skills of a trenchant social historian with the unabashed ardor of a sports fan to present an overview of sports as played, watched, and fervently followed by North Carolinians. It has been only in the last two decades that social and cultural historians have begun to take a serious look at America's sports history. Mr. Sumner has contributed to that new field with articles in the *North Carolina Historical Review* and other scholarly journals. A graduate of Duke University who earned an M.A. in history from North Carolina State University, he is a research historian for the State Historic Preservation Office of the North Carolina Division of Archives and History.

Special thanks are due Robert M. Topkins, who edited the manuscript and skillfully guided the booklet through press; Trudy M. Rayfield, who entered the manuscript in a microcomputer and encoded it for typesetting; and Kathleen B. Wyche, who designed the cover.

Jeffrey J. Crow
Historical Publications Administrator

January, 1990

ACKNOWLEDGMENTS

The author acknowledges the assistance of the Historical Publications Section of the Division of Archives and History, particularly Robert M. Topkins, and the following individuals: Robert G. Anthony, Jr., Raymond L. Beck, David F. Chrisman, Bob Gill, William C. Harris, Michael R. Hill, William E. King, Angela Lumpkin, Stephen E. Massengill, Joe A. Mobley, Elizabeth Reid Murray, Roy Parker, Jr., Marianne D. Wason, and Janice C. Williams.

I. The Colonial Period

Life in colonial North Carolina was not all dull tedium. North Carolinians in this period could and did occupy their leisure time in a variety of recreations and diversions. Among these were a number of early folk sports. Compared to their twentieth-century counterparts, these sports were rudimentary and unformed, lacking the structure and formality that later would come to characterize the North Carolina sporting scene. Yet these sports, crude as they were, made up for their lack of cohesion with an enthusiasm and vigor characteristic of colonial society.

An influx of settlers in the middle part of the eighteenth century, many of whom arrived by way of the Great Wagon Road, helped make North Carolina one of the more populous of Britain's colonies. Yet this population was scattered and overwhelmingly rural. The colony lacked an urban center such as Charleston or Baltimore to give focus to its cultural, social, and recreational life. The poor quality of North Carolina's roads and other means of transportation exacerbated the isolation of its residents. Colonial society was further fragmented by class distinctions, ethnic divisions, and a persistent east-west rivalry.

The overwhelming majority of North Carolina residents during this period engaged in agriculture. Although a planter aristocracy was beginning to develop, particularly in the northeastern part of the colony, most agriculture was practiced by sturdy yeoman farmers. These farms tended to be self-sufficient, and their owners achieved a reputation for independence, industriousness, parochialism, occasional pugnaciousness, and a general suspicion of government. Cooperative endeavors were likely to be neighborhood activities such as barn raising, corn husking, or quilting bees. The planter class was somewhat better traveled and more cosmopolitan and possessed more leisure time in which to pursue recreational opportunities. The gentry were nonetheless severely constrained by the poor transportation and communication capabilities of the colony.

Leisure pursuits that developed during this period shared a number of aspects that reflected the characteristics and limitations of colonial North Carolina. Sports were individual rather than team, participant rather than spectator. Although some of these attracted onlookers, crowds were small and were not necessarily crucial to the activity. Class distinctions could be seen in a number of sports. Gentry and yeoman alike engaged in horse racing, cockfighting, hunting, and fishing. For the yeoman, however, there was a strongly utilitarian aspect to these pursuits that was not present among the aristocracy. Other activities, such as gouging, were practiced only by the "lower" elements of society.

Sports in this period were largely free from the kind of bureaucratic apparatus that began to characterize such undertakings in the nineteenth century. Rules varied from community to community and from year to year. Activities were informal and frequently spontaneous. Results went largely unrecorded. Court sessions, militia musters, elections, and even the right combination of patrons at the local tavern could all lead to impromptu contests of one type or another. Sports were localized, pitting against each other opponents from the same community or perhaps neighboring communities, but rarely from much further apart. The more formal sports, especially horse racing, were derived from English models, although they were adapted to the conditions of frontier society. Like virtually every other aspect of colonial society, these pursuits were organized for and by white males. Women were tolerated as spectators only under rare circumstances, while blacks—slave or otherwise—were severely limited in their recreational opportunities.

Several aspects of colonial sports were decidedly negative. Sports in North Carolina were frequently rough and even violent. Well into the nineteenth century, visitors were appalled by what they considered the gratuitous cruelty characteristic of North Carolina leisure. Many gatherings, sporting or otherwise, were plagued by brawling, drunkenness, and, most of all, gambling. Participants and spectators wagered on the outcome of virtually every type of activity. Indeed, a case could be made that gambling was the most popular pursuit in colonial North Carolina. It was an activity that crossed class and sectional lines. The colonial legislature made numerous attempts to control "gaming" but was notably unsuccessful.

The gambling fever was particularly endemic in the planter class, many of whom viewed their willingness to bet large sums on the outcome of a horse race, a cockfight, a card game, or a billiard match as a means of validating their membership in an elite leadership group. Philadelphia lawyer Charles Biddle said of Halifax County planter Willie Jones: "In point of talent he was one of the first men in America, but like most Southern gentlemen, was too fond of horse racing and cards to attend much to business." Although this characterization was perhaps overstated, many North Carolina planters were criticized in such terms.

The most popular sport in colonial North Carolina was horse racing, the so-called sport of kings. This activity was enormously popular in England in this period, and it was perhaps only natural that it would become popular in the colonies. The Puritan legacy held the sport in check to some degree in the New England colonies during this period. This was not the case in the South, however, and horse racing was widely practiced even in those areas not primarily settled by the English. The center of colonial horse racing was Virginia, with its powerful planter class and strong cavalier tradition. As a result, horse racing in North Carolina reached its apex in the colony's northern counties that bordered Virginia and had strong commercial and social ties with its northern neighbor.

Horses were universal in colonial North Carolina. Even the rudest farmer strove to own one or two, as they were indispensable for traveling and agricultural pursuits. The first horse race in North Carolina, certainly unrecorded, undoubtedly occurred when two men decided to test the mettle of their steeds. By the 1730s Edenton physician John Brickell could write in his *Natural History of North Carolina*: "Horse-racing they [North Carolinians] are fond of for which they have Race-Paths near each town and in many parts of the Country." The popularity of horse racing can be inferred from the fact that the colonial assembly explicitly exempted the sport from the provisions of a law it enacted in 1764 "to suppress excessive and deceitful gaming."

During this period, in the words of author Manly Wade Wellman, horses raced "more or less haphazardly. Stores at country crossroads, taverns on the edge of hamlets, did duty as highly irregular jockey clubs, and ill trained mounts with reckless riders sometimes drove to fatal accidents as they won or lost." Races were short and were usually run on country roads or crude tracks. The most common distance was one quarter of a mile. Two horses would line up, side by side, and race in a straight line to the finish. A horse that strayed from its designated lane or left the course was disqualified. A friendly, or sometimes not so friendly, wager was common, and passions could be high. Combine this with the crude race course, casual or nonexistent training, and the ready presence of spirituous liquor, and the possibilities for accident and injury were obvious.

Nonetheless, North Carolina gained a reputation for the quality of its quarter racing. Well-known British traveler J. F. D. Smyth observed: "In the Southern part of the colony [Virginia] and in North Carolina they are much addicted to quarter-racing . . . and they have a breed which performs it with astonishing velocity, beating every other for that distance with great ease. . . . I am confident that there is no horse in England nor perhaps in the whole world that can excel them in rapid speed."

Although horse racing was popular with all classes, it was only the gentry who could afford to use horses exclusively for racing and to maintain expensive breeding stock. By the middle of the eighteenth century, planters throughout the South were importing expensive English thoroughbreds. This was particularly common in Maryland and Virginia but was not uncommon in North Carolina, especially in the Roanoke valley region adjacent to Virginia. Enthusiasm for racing brought the best imported horses of the colonial region to the upper South, where they in turn produced the best racehorses. This phenomenon reinforced the differences in bloodlines between the horses owned by the aristocracy and those owned by the yeomen. This tendency increased after the Revolution as serious horse racing became largely the preserve of the elite. One of the most famous imports was Janus, who was brought from England to Virginia as a ten-year-old in 1756. Janus stood from 1772 to 1774 in Northampton County, where he was owned by prominent plantation owner and racer Jeptha Atherton. After briefly returning to Virginia, Janus came back to North Carolina in 1778 under the ownership of Atherton's son-in-law, James Barnes of Halifax County. Janus died in North Carolina in 1780. His numerous offspring were well known for their superior speed and were thus particularly well suited for quarter racing. Preceding Janus as a well-known North Carolina stud horse was Monkey, who stood in the colony from 1748 to 1754. Equally well regarded was Mark Anthony, who stood in Northampton and Halifax counties from 1774 to 1789.

OLD JANUS

IS now very fat, and as active as a Lamb, and stands at *Northampton* Courthouse, *North Carolina*, in Order to cover Mares at forty Shillings a Leap, or four Pounds the Season. The Pasturage, which is under a very good Fence, will be allowed gratis, but I will not be liable for any Mare that may be stolen or get away accidentally. Any Gentleman who thinks proper to send a Servant to see the Mares have Justice done in covering, and feeding with Corn at twelve Shillings and Sixpence a Barrel, shall be accommodated gratis.   (1‖)   J. ATHERTON.

This advertisement for stud service by the renowned racehorse Janus appeared in the March 18, 1773, issue of the *Virginia Gazette*, Janus was then twenty-seven years old. Advertisement courtesy Virginia State Library, Richmond.

The best-known owners of racehorses in colonial North Carolina were Willie Jones and Jeptha Atherton. Jones, a wealthy planter, member of the colonial assembly, and strong advocate of independence from Great Britain, was known throughout Virginia and the Carolinas for the quality of his horses. His best-known racers were Trickem and Paoli. The former took the measure of Atherton's Big Filly in a famous pre-Revolutionary race contested for a prize of 100 hogsheads of tobacco. The Bermuda-born Atherton came up short against Jones on several other occasions. Atherton was also the owner of the well-known Mud Colt. Other prominent devotees of colonial quarter racing included Willie Jones's brother, Allen Jones; Governor Gabriel Johnston; Thomas Eaton of Warren County; William Brinkley of Halifax County; and members of the Browne, Chambers, Crawford, Floyd, Gould, Pucket, Taylor, and Whitaker families. Many of these men resided in the Roanoke area, known as the "Old Race Horse Region." In the remainder of the colony horse racing was even less organized and sophisticated than in that famous horse country. An exception was the New Bern area, which was known for some quality horses, including those owned by Richard Ellis and Abner Nash. The 1769 Sauthier map of New Bern clearly shows a racetrack more substantial than the common quarter-mile courses.

Cockfighting was a popular colonial sport with some similarities to horse racing. It was imported from England, was popular with all classes, and involved careful and selective breeding, usually of gamecocks imported from England or Ireland. It was also characterized by gambling, not only on the part of the bird's owners and handlers but also by interested spectators. Although the rules of a match became more standardized in the nineteenth century, a basic format existed in the colonial period. Two birds, bred and trained for fierceness, were placed in a circular pit. Sharp, steel-pointed gaffs were attached to the birds' shanks. The birds would engage in a short, usually vicious fight that ended when one bird was either dead or unable to continue. During this period cockfighting was relatively free of the opposition that would drive it underground in the nineteenth century.

Equally as violent as cockfighting was a gruesome activity known as "gouging." One part boxing, one part wrestling, and one part a deliberate attempt to maim, gouging gained a peculiar hold on the affections of eighteenth-century North Carolinians, particularly those regarded as being not of the better class. The cruelty of gouging can be inferred from the many attempts to legislate against it. In 1746 Governor Gabriel Johnston spoke out against the "barbarous and inhuman manner of Boxing, which so much prevails among the lower Sort of People." In 1749 the legislature banned attempts to "cut out the Tongue, or pull out the Eyes." Five years later it moved to ban the "slitting of noses, the biting or cutting off of a nose or lip, and the biting or cutting off of any limb or member." One eighteenth-century account lists eye gouging, scratching, bruising, pinching, biting, butting, throttling, tripping, kicking, and dismembering as acceptable conduct. Gouging out an opponent's eye was the preferred manner of gaining victory, however. The use of weapons theoretically was prohibited. The contest ended when one fighter signaled his inability or unwillingness to continue. These crude rules, along with the tendency of opponents to schedule matches days in advance and the fact that participants did not necessarily have grudges against their opponents, distinguished gouging from common brawling.

The most universal recreational activity in colonial North Carolina was hunting. Hunting, of course, was more than just recreation. In certain times and places it was a way of controlling predators. For a guide or commercial hunter it was a business. For almost everyone it was a means of supplying food. Yet, it would be a mistake to assume that hunting was strictly utilitarian for even the most humble yeoman. Hunting was considered a noble and manly activity, and introduction into its mysteries was a rite of passage into manhood for generations of North Carolina boys. Janet Schaw, a young Scotswoman who visited North Carolina shortly before the Revolution, offered an indication of the importance of hunting to the residents when she castigated the typical North Carolina farmer for spending his time "sauntering thro' the woods with a gun" rather than attending to his farm. For planters, hunting was both a sport and a social obligation. It was considered routine hospitality to invite guests to hunt deer or fox. Such hunts, conducted from horseback and accompanied by ceremony and a retinue of servants, were another means by which the gentry sought to set themselves apart from the mass of society.

Fishing was equally universal, although it lacked the social appeal of hunting. Fishing was generally regarded as a more thoughtful activity, the better for meditation and contemplation. Other colonial sports such as wrestling, foot racing, and various ball games were even more informal and unstructured than horse racing, cockfighting, or gouging.

North Carolina's colonial black population, mostly slave, participated in sports only on a limited basis. Many of the large planters who raced horses or engaged in cockfighting used slaves in the breeding, raising, or training of those animals, although not to the extent they were used in the nineteenth century.

Even more isolated were the colony's dwindling number of native Americans. Indians hunted, fished, wrestled, and raced in the same manner as whites, but in general they competed only against each other. Athletic competition between Indians and white settlers was apparently sporadic. Indian sport frequently involved a religious aspect absent from the secular sports of the European settlers.

Several Indian games were quite sophisticated. The best known was a highly ritualized but violent team ball game in which players used sticks to drive a ball through a goal. Virtually every Indian tribe played this game, which was known by several names. The most serious contests involved competing villages and were characterized by heavy gambling. This game evolved into the modern sport of lacrosse. In an Indian sport called Chungke, two individuals (sometimes teams) hurled a smooth stone across a square piece of ground and then attempted to throw a pole near the spot where the stone landed. In 1775 Indian trader and author James Adair reported that Indians were "much addicted to this game." The stones were highly prized and were passed from generation to generation.

North Carolina's first formal sports organization was the Wilmington Jockey Club, founded in 1774 and modeled after the Charleston Jockey Club, which had been established in 1734. It is perhaps not surprising that

Wilmington was the site of the first such club. According to colonial Wilmington resident Peter Dubois: "I live very much retired for want of a social set, who will drink claret and smoke tobacco till four in the morning; the gentlemen of this town [could] be so if they pleased but an intolerable itch for gaming prevails in all companies." Of course, the same might be said of other communities. Jockey clubs, which became common in the early eighteenth century, primarily as social organizations, did provide some structure to such gentlemanly activities as horse racing and cockfighting. The Wilmington Jockey Club was shut down almost as soon as it opened. In 1774 the Continental Congress, anticipating the continuation of difficulties with England, asked the colonists to forgo "every species of extravagance and dissipation . . . especially all horse racing and all kinds of gaming, [and] cockfighting." The Wilmington Jockey Club nonetheless announced plans to hold a series of horse races. The Wilmington Committee of Safety responded in no uncertain terms:

as a friend to your country, we have no doubt but you [the members of the club] will readily relinquish an amusement that however laudable in other respects, is certainly attended with considerable expense, and even destruction to many individuals; and may very justly be condemned at a time when frugality should be one of our leading virtues. . . . He only is the determined patriot who willingly sacrifices his pleasures on the altar of freedom.

The Wilmington races were not held. Although there were a few exceptions, sporting endeavors generally came to a standstill during the Revolution, either because of patriotism or lack of opportunity.

II: 1781-1865

In many respects independence had little effect on the recreational habits of the average North Carolinian. The state of North Carolina, like the colony of North Carolina, was a relatively backward and rural agricultural society whose cultural and social stagnation in the first third of the nineteenth century led to such derisive nicknames as "The Rip Van Winkle State" or "The Ireland of the Americas." North Carolina remained isolated and provincial, although improved transportation and communication would begin to ameliorate this condition in the years just prior to the Civil War. The sports of the turf and field—horse racing, cockfighting, hunting, and fishing—remained widespread and perhaps grew in popularity. Gouging was still popular well into the early nineteenth century but declined in the late antebellum period. Sports continued to be predominantly individual and participant oriented, although informal team sports began to make an impact during this period. The negative aspects of sport continued to plague the state, as many observers categorized North Carolinians as violent and brutal. The events of the watershed year of 1835—a state constitutional convention and the unfolding of an era of progress—had little immediate effect on the state's sporting community, with the exception of improved transportation. Historian Hugh Lefler has written: "So slow is the process of the social evolution of a people that the notable development of wealth, trade, education, political democracy, and religious organization after 1835 had not radically changed the pattern of North Carolina by 1860." This also applied largely to sports.

There were some changes, however. Horse racing and, to a lesser extent, cockfighting became more sophisticated and formal. In these sports North Carolina became part of a larger geographic community, with increasingly standardized modes of competing, training, and breeding. During this period the sporting community also encountered stronger opposition than it had faced during the colonial period. The religious enthusiasms of the early nineteenth century focused opposition to a number of activities. Horse racing escaped these sentiments largely unscathed. Cockfighting, on the other hand, was increasingly forced underground, while the decline of gouging can be attributed at least in part to the increasing distaste many North Carolinians felt toward its excesses.

There was some feeling after the Revolution that horse racing was a residue of British dominance and was therefore undesirable. This thinking did not take hold, however, and the sport made a remarkably quick recovery. In 1787 Philadelphian William Attmore visited North Carolina. While in New Bern Attmore was subjected to so much horse racing that he was moved to write: "I have attended the Races yesterday and today rather from motives of curiosity than any love to this Amusement, and think I shall hardly be prevailed on to go ten Steps in future to see any Horse Race." Attmore's journal gives a vivid account of North Carolina horse racing in the late eighteenth century. Attmore complained that the sport was harmful to the well-being of the state inasmuch as "Large numbers of people are drawn from their business, occupations and labour." He noted that "much quarreling, wrangling, Anger, Swearing & Drinking is created and takes place, I saw it . . . prevalent from the highest to the lowest—I saw white Boys, and Negroes eagerly betting ½ a quart of Rum, a drink of Grog &c, as well as Gentlemen betting high." Attmore's journal also testified to the danger that was an ever-present part of racing: "One of the Riders, a Negroe boy, who rid [sic] one of the Horses yesterday, was, while at full speed thrown from his Horse, by a Cow being in the Road and the Horse driving against her in the hurry of the Race—the poor Lad was badly hurt in the Head and bled much." He also described a race in which out-of-control horses veered into a crowd, causing injuries. Thus Attmore touched on three of the most prominent characteristics of eighteenth-century horse racing: its popularity, the prevalence of gambling and drinking, and the attendant danger.

William Attmore observed horse racing at a time when it still retained many of its colonial characteristics. In the nineteenth century the sport lost much of this crudeness. Throughout the nineteenth century, up to the beginning of the Civil War, horse racing increased in popularity, quality, and organizational complexity, becoming the state's first spectator sport. This was also the case nationwide, although in some northern locales harness racing paralleled or even preceded thoroughbred racing in this development. This did not happen in the South, however, where generally poor roads handicapped the development of carriage travel and left riding on horseback the preferred mode of transportation and recreation.

After the Revolution quarter-mile racing gave way to longer, more demanding contests. The colonial point-to-point straight-line courses evolved toward oval or, less often, circular courses in which the finish line was at or near the starting line. This change allowed the owners and breeders of horses a better opportunity to demonstrate the fruits of their endeavors. It also allowed more horses to participate in a given race. Most importantly, it allowed spectators situated near the start/finish line to view the beginning of a race, the conclusion of a race, and a substantial portion of the middle of a race, which obviously was not the case in quarter racing. This modification was essential for the development of horse racing as a spectator sport.

During the eighteenth century, horse racing began developing a bureaucracy. The Wilmington Jockey Club was joined by similar organizations in such communities as Charlotte, Pittsboro, Jackson, Salisbury, Warrenton, Tarboro, Raleigh, and many others. Like the Wilmington organization, these clubs were primarily social in nature. They offered places to which the gentlemen of a community could retire for some sociable relaxation, some pleasant drinking among equals, and perhaps a friendly game of cards. Yet these clubs also were instrumental in creating

An annual subscription card for the spring, 1833, races held at the Jackson Jockey Club in Northampton County. Card courtesy Henry W. Lewis, Pittsboro.

race courses, organizing races, and standardizing rules and purses. They were useful places to exchange information on training, breeding, and strategy. For example, the constitution of the Salisbury Jockey Club, "taking into consideration the advantages experienced in other parts of the country from a good breed of horses and wishing to encourage the same," established no fewer than sixteen regulations relating to horse racing. These rules addressed such concerns as the fair weight to be carried by horses of different ages, length of races, certification of ages, proper attire of jockeys, distribution of purses, and a code of conduct for riders. Many horse owners subscribed to such national racing journals as *American Turf Register*, founded in 1829, and the *Spirit of the Times*, founded in 1831. Local newspapers gave horse racing attention and respect not afforded other sports. As breeding and racing became more important and more lucrative, the value of detailed record keeping—both of breeding lines and major races—became more pronounced. Horse racing thus became the first sport in which quantification was important.

As in the colonial period, the center of North Carolina horse racing in the late eighteenth and early nineteenth centuries was a group of counties that bordered on Virginia, in particular Warren, Halifax, and Northampton counties. The leading men in the sport in this period included Marmaduke Johnson, his son William Ransom Johnson, and James Turner, governor of North Carolina from 1802 until 1805, all from Warren County. From Halifax County Willie Jones and his brother Allen Jones, General Stephen Carney, John Hamilton, John Drew, and John Dawson were prominent horse racers. In Northampton County the leaders of the sport were Jeptha Atherton and his sons Jesse and Wade, and William Amis.

Perhaps the most influential of these was prominent Warren County planter Marmaduke Johnson. According to local tradition, Johnson was introduced to the sport when his carriage driver unhitched a mare and surreptitiously entered her in a local race. Rather than punish the servant, Johnson became fascinated with racing. He built a quarter-mile track on his property and gradually expanded it into an oval course of about one mile in length. Johnson purchased fine and expensive breeding stock, promoted and supported racing, and helped make Warrenton the center of the sport in North Carolina. His son, William Ransom Johnson, born in 1782, became interested in horses at an early age and quickly demonstrated remarkable skill and judgment on the subject. William Ransom Johnson represented Warren County in the North Carolina General Assembly off and on from 1807 until 1814. He moved to Petersburg, Virginia, about 1816. He served in the Virginia House of Delegates and the state Senate at various times between 1818 and 1837. Johnson was known as the "Napoleon of the Turf" and is regarded as the leading American turfman of his generation. Unlike many of his contemporaries, he was more interested in training and racing than in breeding.

Johnson was one of a number of owners of Sir Archie, the best-known racehorse in North Carolina history and one of the leading United States thoroughbreds of the nineteenth century. Sir Archie, who was originally known as Robert Burns, was foaled in Cumberland County, Virginia, in 1805. His father was Diomed and his mother Castianira. Diomed, a notable English import, was the winner of the first English Derby in 1780.

In 1798 he came to Virginia and there sired a number of successful racers. Sir Archie's first co-owners were Archie Randolph and John Tayloe III. Tayloe, whose Mount Airy plantation was one of Virginia's finest, was a keen observer of horses. His failure to recognize the quality of Sir Archie has perplexed observers ever since. In 1807 Ralph Wormeley purchased Sir Archie and unwisely entered the horse in a Richmond race despite the fact that the animal had recently undergone a serious bout with distemper. The out-of-condition three-year-old was defeated twice. The astute Johnson, however, saw something he liked in the young thoroughbred and purchased him from Wormeley for $1,500.

Johnson took Sir Archie to Warren County and began to train him for the 1808 Virginia racing season. By this time the short quarter-mile races of the colonial period had given way to arduous four-mile races, the so-called "Heroic Distance." To complicate matters even more, many big races were run in heats, meaning the thoroughbreds might be forced to run two-, three-, or even more four-mile heats in the course of a grueling afternoon. Sir Archie, conditioned by Johnson and his English-born trainer Arthur Taylor, was entered in the spring Post Stakes race in Richmond. The horse won this race in impressive fashion. The following week he raced again at Newmarket, near Petersburg, and was narrowly beaten by Wrangler (also a son of Diomed). Sir Archie next raced at the Fairfield Jockey Club, where he soundly defeated the cream of the Virginia racing crop, including Wrangler. Later that fall he again won impressively, this time in Richmond.

In one season Sir Archie had demolished the best racehorses Virginia had to offer. He had one race left, and it would be his only race on North Carolina soil. Johnson matched him against Blank, owned by General Stephen Carney. Blank had also just completed a successful season in Virginia. The two horses' schedules did not overlap, however, and this would be their only meeting. The race, held at the Scotland Neck course in Halifax County, was the most famous horse race ever held in North Carolina. Sir Archie won two four-mile heats over his game but overmatched opponent. In the first heat his four-mile time of 7 minutes 52 seconds was the fastest recorded by a southern horse to that date. This would be the only defeat of Blank's career.

With this devastating victory Sir Archie had run out of opponents. Johnson, claiming that "Sir Archie is the best horse I ever saw," offered to run his horse against any thoroughbred in the world for $5,000 or $10,000. He had no takers. When this became apparent, Johnson, who as mentioned was primarily interested in racing, agreed to sell Sir Archie to General William R. Davie for $5,000. Davie, a Revolutionary War hero and former governor, was one of the state's first citizens. He had little to do with the horse, however, turning him over to his ill-starred son, Allen Davie. Allen Davie possessed an enthusiasm for card playing that was, unfortunately, not matched by comparable skill and thus was frequently

The great racehorse Sir Archie. Engraving from Henry William Herbert, *Frank Forester's Horse and Horsemanship* (New York: Stringer and Townsend, 2 volumes, 1857), I, opposite 122.

in debt. Davie was forced to lease Sir Archie, ironically, to William Ransom Johnson and eventually sold him to William Amis, one of his creditors, whose Northampton County plantation was known as Mowfield. Amis obtained Sir Archie from Davie in 1816. The horse stood at stud at Mowfield until 1831, two years before his death.

Sir Archie was phenomenally successful at stud. Called the "Foundation Sire of the American Thoroughbred," he sired some 400 sons and daughters. While at Mowfield he cleared an estimated $76,000 in stud fees for the Amis family. His offspring included such successful racers as Timoleon, Sir Charles, Henry, Marion, Bertram, Lady Lightfoot, and Reality. Lexington, considered the finest racer of the late antebellum period, was a great-grandson. Such successful twentieth-century horses as Man o' War, Gallant Fox, War Admiral, and Native Dancer trace their lineage to Sir Archie. Sir Archie and his get were so successful that in 1827 clubs in Washington, D.C., and Baltimore limited some races to horses owned or trained north of the York River, with the explanation that "We are afraid that our friends in North Carolina are displeased at our . . . having excluded the Roanoke Racers. . . . Do they not perceive that in so doing our Clubs pay them the compliment of considering them invincible?"

Despite the success of Sir Archie and his progeny, Virginia, South Carolina, and Maryland retained their leadership in southern racing. Even the best of the Sir Archies, as many of his offspring came to be known, had to race outside North Carolina to attain regional or national acclaim. Indeed, many of them were owned by Virginians, South Carolinians, or even New Yorkers. Nonetheless, several of the best-known Sir Archies had North Carolina connections. Timoleon, a formidable racer with victories in thirteen of his fifteen career starts, was owned for a period by William Ransom Johnson's brother, Robert Johnson of Warren County, and was able to win races in Warrenton, Halifax, and Scotland Neck. Timoleon was the father of Boston and the grandfather of Lexington, two major antebellum thoroughbreds. Walk-in-the-Water, first owned by Jared Weaver and later by Wade Bynum, and Sir Charles, foaled at the plantation of Peyton Maughan of Halifax County, were also nationally prominent racers.

Although the Roanoke region dominated the sport in North Carolina, there was fine horse racing in other sections of the state. Salisbury was the center of the sport in the West. The Salisbury Jockey Club was founded in 1804 under the leadership of John Steele, John McClellan, and John Fulton. The most important races were held at a track on the John Steele plantation during the Christmas season and were followed by a gala Jockey Club ball. Further west, horse racing was introduced to the mountains by the McDowells of Revolutionary War fame, the Carsons, Robert Love, and James Murphy, all of Burke County. In the 1780s, according to local tradition, a young Salisbury lawyer named Andrew Jackson came to the mountains to race against the McDowells. By the 1830s a more formal racetrack was located on the Quaker Meadows property of Charles McDowell in Burke County. Even in this remote area, several offspring of Sir Archie were found.

The State Jockey Club was founded near Raleigh in 1838 under the leadership of Major David McDaniel, Robert Haywood, William Holloman, Walter Otey, John Bryan, and Beverly Daniel. The ambitious club announced that it intended to become the "Central Race Course of the Union," a goal it never attained. Beginning in 1853, the club held races at the annual State Fair on grounds then located in east Raleigh. McDaniel figured in one of the more gruesome episodes in the state's horse-racing history. In May, 1839, his stables were set ablaze, apparently by an unknown arsonist. The fire resulted in the death of McDaniel's prize thoroughbred, Red Wasp.

Wilmington, the site of the state's first jockey club, was a center of the sport in the southeast portion of the state. Equally important was New Bern. By the 1820s the Craven County Jockey Club held a gala three days of racing at the beginning of every May. In most parts of the state horse racing was a staple of the county fairs, which began in the late antebellum period.

Throughout this period horse racing was unsuccessfully attacked by some critics as an aristocratic conceit, a waste of valuable time and money, and a frivolous diversion. Economic downturns such as the Panic of 1837 stalled the sport temporarily. By the 1850s the generally harmonious relations between northern and southern horse owners were being strained by the dark clouds of slavery and secession. Yet, despite these problems there is little question that horse racing was the most important sport in antebellum North Carolina.

Cockfighting increased in popularity during the nineteenth century despite increasing attempts to control it. Many churchgoers found the sport barbarous. Several unsuccessful attempts were made to ban cockfighting statewide, while some communities, such as Salisbury, did succeed in moving it outside their town limits. By about 1815 the state's newspapers refused to publish advertisements for cockfights.

Despite this opposition, the visceral appeal of two birds engaged in a life-or-death struggle had countless devotees. Like horse racing, the activity increased in sophistication and organization throughout this

Cockfights were occasionally accompanied by heated exchanges, and even outright combat, between the birds' owners. Engraving from Porte Crayon (pseud. David Hunter Strother), "North Carolina Illustrated," Part II, *Harper's New Monthly Magazine* XIV (May, 1857), 753.

period. Indeed, the same jockey clubs that promoted horse racing had many members who were avid cockfighters. By the Civil War a fairly well-defined cockfighting season existed, running from around Thanksgiving to the Fourth of July. The birds were classified by weight and were bred, trained, and conditioned with all the fervor applied to the care of thoroughbred racehorses. Fights tended to be short and savage. Bred and trained for ferocity, many birds would fight to the death. Gambling, brawling, and excessive consumption of alcohol continued to characterize and, in the opinion of some, mar the event.

The best-known antebellum breeder of birds was Nash County planter Nick Arrington. One visitor to the Arrington estate "was greeted by such a crowing of cocks as he had never heard in all his life before. Hundreds of cocks seemed to be crowing simultaneously and unceasingly. The air was resonant with their shrill notes, challenging and replying in fierce and eager tone." Arrington is reputed to have won a "main" (a series of matches) of three hundred cocks in Memphis for a stake of $5,000. Another Arrington story holds that his birds were victorious over the birds of Mexican president Santa Ana in a contest decided on a neutral site— aboard two steamboats in the Gulf of Mexico.

Advocates of cockfighting might possibly have answered their critics with the words of noted author and traveler David Hunter Strother, who wrote under the name of Porte Crayon. Visiting an unnamed eastern North Carolina community shortly before the Civil War, Strother happened upon a cockfight. He declared that "there is an absurd prejudice existing at the present day against this elegant sport." Strother further maintained that "the people one meets at such places are, in all respects, the same as those who, under our admirable system, play the most prominent part in the government of the country."

Horse racing and cockfighting had the strong support of the gentry, or at least elements of this class. This was not the case with gouging, which remained an activity of the yeoman class. By the middle part of the nineteenth century it had brought a certain notoriety to the state, to the embarrassment of many North Carolinians. Yet, gouging persisted in its hold on backwoods and lower-class Tar Heels because, in the words of historian Elliot Gorn, it "reinforced the daily truth that life was brutal, guided only by the logic of superior nerve, power, and cunning."

In the early days of the Republic it was widely stated that the foremost proponents of rough-and-tumble fighting resided in Virginia, Georgia, and the Carolinas. Observers such as Jedediah Morse in *American Universal Geography* (1793), Isaac Weld in *Travels through the States of North America* (1800), and Charles Janson in *The Stranger in America* (1807) all gave North Carolina a high rank in gouging. Weld wrote: "In the Carolinas and Georgia, I have been credibly assured, that the people are still more depraved in this respect than in Virginia and that in some parts of these states, every third or fourth man appears with one eye."

16

In a gouging contest, virtually anything was permitted, including butting, depicted here. Engraving from Harden E. Taliaferro, *Fisher's River (North Carolina) Scenes and Characters* . . . (New York: Harper and Brothers, 1859), 200.

Other observers told of one-eyed men, of gougers who sharpened their nails, even of gougers who filed their teeth. Janson, on a visit to Georgia, witnessed a contest between North Carolinian John Butler and an unnamed Georgian. Janson observed that the two men were "fast clinched by the hair, and their thumbs endeavoring to force a passage into each other's eyes; while several of the bystanders were betting upon the first eye to be turned out of its socket. . . . At length they fell to the ground and in an instant the uppermost sprung up with his antagonist's eye in his hand!!! The savage crowd applauded, while, sick with horror, we galloped away from the infernal scene." Butler lost the contest, his eye, and "the honor of the state."

Cockfighting and gouging were not the only North Carolina sports to meet with censure from travelers. Another "sport" known for its casual cruelty was gander pulling. In this activity a gander was suspended by his feet from a tree. His neck was then tallowed. Contestants paid for chances to ride on horseback under the bird and attempt to pull his neck off. The gander would be alive when this procedure began. The usual inebriation of the contestants could prolong the bird's agony to an hour or more before the contest ended. Like other, similar endeavors, gander pulling was accompanied by gambling and drinking. For some reason, it became particularly associated with Easter. Contests would be advertised well in advance, and "the arrival of this period [was] for some weeks anticipated with rapture." Many North Carolinians agreed with Thomas Henderson, who in 1811 wrote: "I cannot help recommending this as a most delightful amusement to all lovers of fun."

Gander pulls were among a number of folk sports frequently held at taverns. In the overwhelmingly rural society of antebellum North Carolina, the tavern was an important meeting place. During holidays, militia musters, elections, court days, or similar occasions the local tavern became the community focal point. The tavern could be the site of horse races deemed too crude for the fancy jockey clubs of the gentry, cockfights, gouging or wrestling matches, gander pulls, shooting matches, foot racing, billiards, jumping, fives, bandy, rounders, and early forms of football.

Several of these games were crude prototypes of twentieth-century sports. Modern football, baseball, soccer, golf, and tennis all evolved out of such activities. Fives was a type of tennis played with a long-handled "fives bat." Rounders and its city cousin, townball, were the sports from which baseball evolved in New York in the 1840s. Bandy, also called shinny, was an early team sport filled with action, excitement, and a high number of injuries. It bore some resemblance to field hockey. There were a number of football-like sports that were variations on the theme of two teams attempting to kick a ball across a line or into a goal. Early forms of golf and bowling also appeared in the state. All of these sports were relatively unstructured, impromptu activities of transitory local significance.

Sports in the state's antebellum schools and academies were likewise unstructured. Organized sports were not the focal point of school life they later became. On the contrary, the attitude of many school administrators toward sports ranged from indifference to outright hostility. In 1799 officials at the University of North Carolina explicitly prohibited students from participating in horse racing, cockfighting, hunting, or fishing and placed restrictions on the playing of bandy. These prohibitions were modified throughout the early nineteenth century. Nonetheless, schools lacked gymnasiums and formal playing fields, and sporting activities were unsupervised and informal.

Among the more popular school sports were hunting, fishing, townball, and particularly bandy. Bandy was played with such enthusiasm that it practically invited injury. J. R. Cole, a Trinity College student just before the Civil War, described games of bandy with thirty to forty students: "as the big hard ball is thrown up or down, see them rush up to it with uplifted clubs, and strike right and left crying 'shin on your side' and see them jump into the air to avoid a savage blow, and the ball is knocked whirling, and all rush for it, and sticks fly, and hands are hurt, and limbs are bruised, and heads are struck." Cole also wrote that school president Braxton Craven encouraged recreational activities "considered helpful to students." More typical, perhaps, was the attitude of William Chaffin, who operated an academy in Stokes County. In 1848 Chaffin published rules that listed forty-seven offenses punishable by from one to ten lashes. The offenses and punishments included fighting, 5 lashes; telling lies, 7 lashes; absent without permission, 4 lashes; and drinking spirituous liquors, 8 lashes. The three most serious violations, all punishable by 10 lashes, were playing cards, misbehaving to girls, and playing bandy. Despite the apparent roughness of bandy, it is remarkable that playing a game was deemed more harmful to schoolchildren than drinking alcohol.

Hunting and fishing remained almost universal activities for antebellum North Carolina males, regardless of class or social standing. Virtually every household owned guns, hunting dogs, and fishing gear. As the state became less of a frontier, it became necessary to impose some limits on hunting, such as laws enacted in 1784 and 1810 to control deer hunting. These laws were not considered overly burdensome, however, and for many the state was a hunter's paradise. Deer, raccoon, opossum, turkey, duck, and quail were among the animals hunted for food and sport.

William Attmore, the critic of horse racing, spent about as much time hunting deer while in North Carolina as he did attending races. He considered hunting a pleasurable diversion and offered it none of the criticism he leveled at racing. For many plantation owners, large and elaborate hunts were a social obligation. A few held formal fox hunts with horses, dogs, and a retinue of following slaves. Most hunting took place in the fall and winter, when agricultural obligations were less pressing.

This early duck-hunting scene took place at the "Mouth of the Pasquotank River, Albemarle Sound." Engraving from private collection.

For many, hunting was more than a recreation or a way to obtain food. For its most vocal proponents, hunting was a means of obtaining physical fitness, promoting manliness, and teaching moral fiber. South Carolinian William Elliott, whose *Carolina Sports by Land and Water* was an important primer for antebellum hunters, wrote: "of all the associates who have acted with me in field sports, and were interested enough to excel in them, not one has been touched with the vice of gaming! Men of fortune, men of leisure, peculiarly exposed, from their social position, to this most demoralizing vice, have been completely exempt from it." Elliot ascribed this good fortune to the habits of hunting: punctuality, patience, observation, sagacity, and other positive characteristics.

Fishing was likewise a sport, a recreation, and in some areas a business, particularly in the eastern part of the state. It was widely maintained that fishing was a natural right of man and that access to rivers, lakes, and ponds should not be arbitrarily denied or impeded by such means as dams or trees. For the yeoman, fishing was particularly attractive since it was inexpensive, required little equipment, and could be engaged in on short notice.

During a visit to North Carolina in 1857, artist Porte Crayon created this sketch of a typical fisherman. Engraving from Porte Crayon, "North Carolina Illustrated," Part I, *Harper's New Monthly Magazine*, XIV (March, 1857), 444.

Hunting and fishing were also popular with the state's black population. Indeed, in spite of the very serious restrictions placed on North Carolina's slaves and free blacks, they managed to participate in a variety of recreational activities. By the advent of the Civil War approximately one third of the state's one million inhabitants were blacks. About thirty thousand of them were free blacks, one of the largest such totals in the South.

North Carolina's slaves did have some leisure time. Most slave owners recognized, whether from altruism, enlightened self-interest, or community censure, that some time for recreation was essential for the smooth running of the plantation or farm. Many plantations gave field hands Saturday afternoons off, and Sunday was virtually a universal day of rest. Holidays, especially Christmas, were important sources of leisure time. Particularly bad weather could also temporarily reduce work obligations, as could the relatively slack period following harvest. Sports were considered a way to lighten the slave's burden, relieve boredom, and give the bondsman a rare chance to achieve personal satisfaction. Since slaves generally had more control over their recreational and social life than other aspects of their life, sports were a means of achieving some sense of community. However, inasmuch as the slave owner could withdraw these privileges at any time, it was also a means of social control and possibly a way of restraining the slave's rebellious tendencies.

The most popular slave recreational activities were dancing and singing. Hunting and fishing were the most popular sports. Technically, the use of guns by slaves was severely limited. In practice this was not always the case as some slave owners rewarded particularly loyal or productive slaves by allowing hunting privileges (with the permission of the county court). Slaves denied access to guns used traps, snares, and even rocks to capture game. North Carolina slave narratives are full of references to hunting. Zeb Crowder, for example, remembered "Marster 'lowed my daddy ter hunt wid a gun and he killed a lot of rabbits, sqirrels, an' game." John Smith recalled: "I caught rabbits, coons, an' possums wid dogs. Dey fared but middlin' pore wid us." Raccoons and opossums appeared to be especially popular fare. Fishing was less problematic since fishing gear in the hands of a slave was not considered a threat. In addition to the recreational advantages of fishing, some slaves were able to obtain money by commercial fishing, to the occasional consternation of whites such as the fifty-six New Bern residents who complained to the 1831 legislature that they had been "much injured by large gangs of slaves" engaged in commercial fishing.

In addition to hunting and fishing, slaves took part in foot races, wrestling, jumping, and other physical activities. Slave owners who engaged in horse racing or cockfighting made liberal use of servants. Those planters who raced horses on the largest scale made especial use of slaves as jockeys, trainers, or grooms. Sir Archie, for example, benefited much from the care and attention of his slave groom Uncle Hardy. Willie Jones, prominent horse racer of the colonial and early Federal era, made equally good use of Austin Curtis Jones, who was called "the best quarter horse jockey, trainer and groom in the country." Slaves such as Austin Curtis Jones and Uncle Hardy who were able to bring prestige and profit to their owners through the medium of sport constituted a privileged class in the slave community. Of course, they were relatively few in number. For most North Carolina slaves, sports and recreation offered more modest goals.

The state's free blacks were regarded as a threat to the "contentment" of the slave population. For this reason, relationships between free blacks and slaves were carefully regulated. Free blacks were forbidden to marry slaves, although this prohibition was not always strictly enforced. Other social contact was regulated, as were financial relationships. In the words of historian John Hope Franklin, "The free Negro's opportunities for social contact were so meager that dancing, drinking, gaming, and the like were important factors in his social life." Denied reasonable contact with the slave community, the free black was confined to a small group and had relatively limited recreational opportunities. The free black did have better access to guns than did slaves, making it easier to hunt. There are also accounts of free blacks engaging in cockfighting, gouging, and other sports. In general, however, the free black was greatly underrepresented in the state's antebellum sporting life.

Women were even less well represented in the sporting scene. Although some women achieved proficiency with a hunting rifle or in riding a horse, such examples were rare. Upper-class women were considered too delicate and refined for the crude sports of the time, while women of more modest means were expected to find recreation in such utilitarian pursuits as quilting bees. Even as spectators, women were in short supply. Only horse racing attracted women spectators to any major extent. Even then women were generally regarded only as part of the social fabric of fair week, mere accessories to the important business of racing thoroughbreds.

III: 1865-1900

The period from 1865 until 1900 was a time of transition from the relatively informal, unstructured folk games of the antebellum period to the highly organized spectator sports of the twentieth century. During this period horse racing and cockfighting declined in popularity but still retained some following. Other antebellum activities such as gouging or gander pulling disappeared after the war. Modern sports such as baseball, football, tennis, and golf evolved out of crude precursors, with baseball gaining a particularly strong hold on North Carolinians.

A more fundamental change came in the increased perception that sports were beneficial to participants and to society as a whole. Although some held on to the view that sports were a frivolous waste of time at best and a dangerous vice at worst, increasingly large numbers of Tar Heels were of the opinion that sports had value and worth in providing recreation and relaxation and, more importantly, inculcating such worthy values as hard work, fair play, decency, honor, courage, and "manliness." Although this new viewpoint was evident in many areas of North Carolina life, it was most obvious on the state's colleges, where formal athletic programs were a part of most campuses by the end of the century.

The last quarter of the nineteenth century saw a dramatic increase in bureaucracy and organization. Such national sporting associations as the Intercollegiate Association of Amateur Athletics (1875), the American Intercollegiate Football Association (1876), the United States Lawn Tennis Association (1881), the American Amateur Association (1888), and the Amateur Golf Association of the United States (1891) were founded during this period. Local counterparts of these national associations were established in North Carolina. Many towns had athletic clubs, which were both social organizations and rudimentary sports bureaucracies. Although some of these promoted a variety of sports, many existed only to form baseball teams. Colleges experimented with a variety of approaches to organization, involving different roles for students, faculties, and trustees. These control bodies served a number of valuable functions, including standardization of rules, regulation of conduct, and promotion of their particular sport.

Sports benefited from improvements in transportation and communication. The most obvious of these improvements was the development of the postwar statewide rail network. This system provided relatively easy interurban travel. Town baseball clubs, college athletic teams, and well-to-do sport hunters all used the rails to help break down the state's sporting provincialism. Better transportation enabled the State Fair to become a true statewide institution, particularly after the opening of the fair's much larger second site in west Raleigh in 1873. Although it was designed to promote progressive agriculture rather than recreation, the fair during this period became the center of horse racing in North Carolina, introduced many of the state's citizens to baseball and football, and hosted a number of other sports. At a time when there were few true statewide institutions, the State Fair was an important force for standardization in sports.

Another force for standardization was the state's newspapers. Although the formal sports page did not appear in Tar Heel papers until the early part of the twentieth century, the newspapers' coverage of sports increased dramatically during the latter years of the nineteenth century. The creation of a national telegraphic network, the laying of the Atlantic cable in 1866, and the establishment of the Associated Press were all factors in this increased coverage. Reports of major league baseball games, out-of-state horse races, and European boxing matches all made their way into North Carolina papers. Also founded during this period were a number of national sporting magazines, many of which could be found in Tar Heel sporting circles.

Despite these increases in organization and standardization, North Carolina sports remained predominantly player oriented rather than spectator oriented. Big-time spectator sports depend on urbanization, and—New South rhetoric notwithstanding—North Carolina was overwhelmingly rural in the late nineteenth century. Cities provide population density, a middle class with leisure time, facilities, media attention, and superior transportation—all necessary components for the growth and development of spectator sports. Minor league baseball, the state's first major team spectator sport, did not prosper until well into the twentieth century.

The Civil War devastated horse racing in North Carolina and the rest of the South. The fine blooded stock of the Confederacy became instruments of war, spoils of war, and, all too often, casualties of war. Many of the best breeding centers were overrun by armies, both hostile and friendly, or allowed to deteriorate through inactivity. The plantation system, which supported the most sophisticated southern breeding and racing, was destroyed. Horse racing's center of gravity moved north to Kentucky, Maryland, and New York, leaving the South with a new second-rate status. Although horse racing remained popular in North Carolina, the quality of the sport declined and the state was relatively unimportant in a national context. Such antebellum racing centers as Warrenton tried in vain to resurrect the sport in the postwar era. In Northampton County racing retained a measure of its earlier popularity under the influence of such prominent patrons as Thomas Goode Tucker and Confederate hero and United States Senator Matt W. Ransom.

The State Fair and local county fairs became the centers of horse racing in North Carolina. Harness racing came to equal thoroughbred racing in popularity at the various fairs during the 1870s. Such prominent North Carolinians as George Harden and Bennehan Cameron of Durham County, L. Banks Holt of Alamance County, and W. P. Batchelor of Wake County routinely raced their horses at the State Fair. The fair also managed to attract horses from such states as New York, Virginia, Maryland, and South Carolina. These horses were rarely the cream of the crop, however. In 1895 one expert wrote Bennehan Cameron, then serving as president of the Agricultural Society: "The greatest objection to racing in North Carolina has all ways been the smallness of the purses, incompetent judges, . . . and the fair's bad track." With such a reputation, it is little wonder that North Carolina horse racing remained second rate. This situation worsened during the financial crisis caused by the Panic of 1893. A determined effort by Bennehan Cameron during his one year in charge of the fair succeeded in stabilizing a deteriorating situation. Cameron was particularly successful in upgrading the quality of judging at the fair but was notably unsuccessful in improving the meager purses that continued to keep the best horses away. Few North Carolina horses achieved national fame during this period. Probably the best known was Pamlico, a trotter owned by W. P. Batchelor of Wake County.

Cockfighting also retained a measure of its prewar popularity but was unable to expand its hold because of unceasing opposition from "polite society." Despite this opposition, the sport continued to find adherents among rich and poor, urban and rural, easterner and westerner. Among the better-known owners of fighting birds were James Norwood of Hillsborough, W. S. Church of Boonville, Ike Rhodes of Wilmington, and George Means of Concord. Means developed a well-known breed of birds known as Red Cubans. One of these birds, Jaybird, reputedly won $10,000 in Mexico in 1899 and retired victorious after twenty-seven fights. Cockfighting remained popular in both Virginia and South Carolina, and interstate mains, in which birds from North Carolina were matched against those of one of its neighbors, were not uncommon. Nonetheless, cockfighting was a sport whose time had passed. It increasingly operated on the periphery of the newly developing sporting society and eventually was driven completely outside the mainstream of that society.

While horse racing and cockfighting struggled to maintain their prewar popularity, other antebellum activities such as bandy, townball, and a number of crude variations of football evolved into such modern sports as baseball, football, golf, and tennis. The most dramatic of these transitions was the rise of baseball to a position of dominance in North Carolina and the rest of the nation.

Baseball evolved from a number of children's bat-and-ball games, including rounders, townball, and one cat. It was first formally organized in the Northeast. The New York Knickerbockers, organized in 1845, are generally recognized as the first baseball club, while Knickerbocker Alexander Cartwright is credited with devising the first written rules for the game. The National Association of Base Ball Players was formed in 1858 with twenty-five teams representing such cities as New York, Baltimore, Washington, and Philadelphia. By the advent of the Civil War a number of modern rules were in place, including the nine-man team, the three-out inning, and the nine-inning game. Contrary to popular belief, baseball was played in some areas of the antebellum South, including New Orleans and Charleston. It was not as common below the Mason-Dixon line as above, however, and it is not clear if the sport was played in North Carolina prior to the Civil War.

The best available evidence suggests that baseball was introduced to North Carolina, along with much but not all of the South, during the Civil War. Troops of both armies played it incessantly behind the lines. The sport was even played with some frequency in the Confederate prison at Salisbury, at least in the relatively benign early days of the facility. Prisoner Charles Carroll Gray, a Union physician from New York, paints an almost idyllic scene in his diary, mentioning plentiful exercise, reading, card playing, and almost daily baseball games in the prison during the spring and summer of 1862. On July 4, 1862, Union prisoners celebrated the holiday with speeches, a reading of the Declaration of Independence, sack races and footraces, and a baseball game in which "the cheers given in the grove were of a sort never before heard in Salisbury." A depiction of Salisbury prison baseball drawn by Major Otto Boetticher is one of the most famous nineteenth-century baseball portraits. But as the war progressed and the prison became horribly overcrowded, baseball gave way to a more basic struggle for survival.

Baseball quickly spread across the state after the war. There are accounts of baseball being played in Asheville in the state's relatively isolated mountain region as early as 1866 on a field known as the "Barn Field" (near present Patton Avenue); a more detailed account exists of games played at the Sand Hill School in Buncombe County beginning in 1868. Residents of Raleigh, Fayetteville, Greensboro, and other communities were playing the sport by the late 1860s. Teams from Pittsboro and Goldsboro introduced baseball at the State Fair in 1873. By the end of the 1870s virtually every community of consequence had one or more teams, not only playing close neighbors but also taking advantage of the state's newly emerging railroad system and playing more distant opponents.

The precise date baseball was first played in North Carolina is not known, but during the Civil War Otto Boetticher, a Union officer from New York, painted this pastoral scene of Union prisoners playing the game in the Confederate prison camp at Salisbury. Photograph of painting from the North Carolina Collection, University of North Carolina Library, Chapel Hill.

More than any other nineteenth-century sport, baseball crossed all lines. Although many of the earliest baseball organizations in the Northeast were composed of gentlemen of the professional class, the game quickly spread to laborers, farmers, and students. In a period during which gloves were not used and balls and bats were frequently homemade, baseball was affordable for anyone. According to its many proponents, baseball's speed and excitement, its blend of teamwork and individuality, and its honor and manliness characterized the strengths of America. That baseball was the national pastime was an axiom by the last quarter of the nineteenth century. In North Carolina baseball was played throughout the state, from the sea to the mountains. It was played by the sons of the elite in the state's colleges, by young businessmen in the small urban communities, by factory and mill laborers, by rural residents, by whites and by blacks. Women, although not participants, frequented baseball games with more regularity than other sports, with the possible exception of horse racing.

The Cincinnati Red Stockings became the first openly all-professional baseball team in 1869. Several major professional leagues were born in the 1870s, including the still-active National League, which was formed in 1876. The first North Carolinian to play in the big leagues apparently was an Alamance County native named Benjamin Rippay, whose successful major league career ran from 1876 until 1888. Rippay played under the pseudonym Charles Wesley Jones. In 1880 Jones became the first player to hit two home runs in a single major league game.

A number of minor leagues were founded in the 1870s and 1880s. The first professional leagues in the South were the 1885 Southern League, with teams in Georgia, Alabama, and Tennessee, and the 1885 Virginia League, which operated irregularly until the early twentieth century. This professional activity had little impact in North Carolina, however. Even the largest towns in the overwhelmingly rural landscape of late nineteenth-century North Carolina were too small to support professional baseball. Tar Heel baseball clubs of this period remained ostensibly amateur, although surreptitious payments to skilled players were not unheard of, marking a transition of sorts from the total amateurism of the early postwar period to the formal minor leagues of the early twentieth century.

Ben Cosby was a baseball player for the Raleigh Athletic baseball club of 1875. The previous October the *Daily Sentinel* (Raleigh) had noted that the Athletics, as well as their opponents, the "Swiftfoot" club, "had donned for the first time their beautiful new uniforms which they had just received from New York, and their fine forms fitted so nicely they presented a splendid appearance." Photograph courtesy North Carolina Museum of History.

Many teams were organized along the lines of a social club. The sport's structure was rather haphazard, lacking leagues, schedules, statistics, provisions for determining champions, and other such later characteristics of the game. Yet, many of the state's small cities and towns had developed fierce baseball rivalries by the end of the century, and a big game could attract partisans who came from miles around, ready not only to cheer their team to victory but also to spend their hard-earned money. Even during the so-called amateur era, baseball was beginning to make a financial impact, however modest.

The development of baseball on the state's college campuses was equally haphazard. Students played the game among themselves for years before attempting any organization. The first teams operated without coaches, without school funds, and occasionally against the opposition of school officials. At North Carolina A&M (now North Carolina State University) for example, baseball players were forced to schedule their practice time around mandatory military drill. Budgets were so scarce and travel restrictions so tight that most colleges were obliged to play high schools or military schools in their immediate area rather than travel to play more distant college competitors.

A constant problem was the academic standing, or lack thereof, of the players. With no firm rules in place, it was not uncommon for schools to place on their teams players of marginal academic standing or, in some cases, professional minor league players. The South's first athletic conference, the Southern Intercollegiate Athletic Association (SIAA), was founded in 1894 with its express purpose being the "development, regulation, and purification of college athletics in the South." Regulations enacted by the league included a transfer rule that required students to have been in residence for one year before attaining eligibility and a rule prohibiting professional summer play. The University of North Carolina, an early member of the SIAA, was an offender of the amateur rules and was suspended from the organization on several occasions; but it was not the only school to be so disciplined. The SIAA was an early precursor of the athletic conferences that came to dominate the college scene in the twentieth century.

The development of football shared some similarities with that of baseball. Football, like the national pastime, evolved from a number of predecessors. Also like baseball, it underwent numerous rules changes before reaching its modern form. Unlike baseball, however, early football did not possess the almost universal appeal of its ball-and-bat cousin. Well into the twentieth century football was largely associated with college campuses. The 1869 Rutgers-Princeton contest is widely regarded as the birth of college football. But in this contest the ball could be advanced only by kicking or heading, making it more the forerunner of soccer than football. An 1874 Harvard-McGill University match first allowed the ball to be advanced by running, making it a more direct prototype.

Faculty recruited from northern schools introduced football to southern colleges. The sport was played informally in North Carolina by the early 1880s. In October, 1888, a team made up entirely of sophomores at the University of North Carolina challenged Wake Forest to a game played at Raleigh during the State Fair. Wake Forest won 6-4 in a contest that featured a potpourri of improvised rules. On Thanksgiving Day, 1888, the University of North Carolina met Trinity College, also at the fairgrounds, in a game played under the accepted rules of intercollegiate football. This was the first "scientific" game of college football played in North Carolina. Trinity president John Franklin Crowell had learned the modern game while a student at Yale and had taught the sport to his students. The well-trained Trinity eleven easily handled the university team in a 16-0 victory. Crowell later wrote: "That single game probably did more than anything else to send into limbo the age-long habit of the condescending attitude with which certain friends of that venerable institution were inclined to look upon . . . Trinity."

On Thanksgiving night, following the game, students from Trinity, UNC, and Wake Forest organized the North Carolina Intercollegiate Football Association. The student-operated league was short-lived because of a series of disputes over player eligibility, scheduling, umpiring, and organizational matters. Nevertheless, it planted in North Carolina a seed that grew throughout the 1890s. Other colleges that formed intercollegiate teams in that decade included North Carolina A&M, Davidson, and Guilford. Several intersectional games of importance took place during that period. The University of Virginia became a common opponent of several North Carolina schools. In 1893 North Carolina traveled north to play Lehigh, receiving a 34-0 defeat in the process. On December 27, 1892, Livingstone College met Biddle Institute (now Johnson C. Smith University) on the Livingstone campus at Salisbury in the first intercollegiate football played anywhere between black colleges. On a bitterly cold day, Livingstone, led by future school president William Trent, won 4-0.

Despite this apparent growth of popularity during the 1890s, it was still a decade of turbulence for the new sport. College eligibility rules were as fluid and controversial in football as in baseball, and the use of professionals and "instant students" was a constant problem. The University of North Carolina dropped football for the academic year of 1890-1891 and reinstated it only under firm faculty control. Trinity College, despite its early successes, discontinued football following the 1894 season at the behest of John Franklin Crowell's successor, John Kilgo. The reason cited for this drastic step was the fear that professionalism might threaten the academic integrity of the school. An equally important factor, however, was opposition to the sport by Methodist leaders who felt that football was undermining the morals of the student body. This view was expressed by the *Raleigh Christian Advocate* when it cited "needless expense, . . . gambling and other immoralities . . . [and] states of excitement subversive of habits of study" as evils of the game. Following the 1895 season Wake Forest joined Trinity on the sidelines as the faculty voted to abolish football, citing professionalism, the bad moral climate of the game, and its expense. Thus, less than a decade after the birth of intercollegiate football in the state, two of the three founders had dropped the sport.

Another problem was finances. Football was not yet a revenue-producing sport, and school administrators begrudged every dollar spent for transportation, equipment, facilities, or other necessities. At North Carolina A&M school trustees, led by prominent New South industrialist Daniel A. Tompkins, succeeded in eliminating football and all other intercollegiate sports at the close of the 1895 season. Only through concerted efforts by students and other supporters of sports were intercollegiate athletics reinstated the following year.

Others criticized football's violence. The forward pass had not yet been incorporated into the game, and contests of this period were characterized by mass formations and brute strength. Poor equipment and a lack of competent coaching added to the injury problem. The death of University of Georgia player Von Gammon from injuries received in an 1897 game against the University of Virginia resulted in cries of protest and institutional soul searching that came close to ending the game in the South. This crisis passed, barely, and by the end of the century football had established a tenuous foothold on the state's intercollegiate athletic scene.

Baseball and football were not the only college sports in the late nineteenth century. Gymnastics made an appearance on several campuses in the 1880s. Both Wake Forest and UNC built gymnasiums in the middle 1880s, and other colleges followed suit. Gymnastics had several things to recommend it. It was safe; it did not attract undesirable or phony students; and, unlike football and baseball, which gradually became the province of elite athletes, it was open to all students, who likewise were free to use school gymnasiums. More importantly, gymnastics was a physical activity deemed acceptable for women and as such served as the starting point for women's college athletics. Despite its popularity, however, gymnastics was purely recreational in this period and did not involve intercollegiate contests.

Tennis was also introduced to college campuses in the 1880s. It was particularly popular at UNC, where the school champions competed against their counterparts from the University of Virginia and Richmond College in 1893. By 1895 UNC boasted fifteen tennis courts and a campuswide tennis association. Track and field events were contested on most campuses, usually as intramural field days, pitting one class against another. It would be the 1900s, however, before meets between schools were held with any regularity. Other college sports in existence during this period include bicycling, lacrosse, and rugby.

Perhaps more important than the number or types of sports engaged in by different schools was the establishment during this period of college and university structures, however crude, for the control of athletics. These structures varied in size and powers, depending on the school. At A&M the Athletic Association was founded in 1895. Comprised of all the students, the association was responsible for financing sports and electing captains and managers; it is generally credited with gaining reconsideration of the trustees' 1895 decision to ban sports. At the University of North Carolina athletics were directed by a three-member committee, with one representative each from the faculty, the graduate students, and the undergraduate students. The committee reported to and was responsible to the faculty. Other schools such as Wake Forest and Davidson gave full control of athletics to the faculty.

Although baseball and, to a lesser extent, football brought a certain amount of democratization to North Carolina athletics, strong class divisions still existed in the state's sports. In addition to horse racing, a number of sports continued to be monopolized by the upper classes. Most notable was the sport of golf, which was introduced, in its modern form, to the state in the 1890s. Like most contemporary sports, golf evolved in the nineteenth century from a number of antecedents. There were several golf courses in the state by the middle 1890s, including the Asheville Golf Club, the Highland Country Club of Fayetteville, and the Hot Springs Country Club of Madison County. But the most important golf activity in the state took place in Pinehurst. In 1895 James Walker Tufts, a wealthy Massachusetts businessman, moved to that small town to begin what ostensibly was to be his retirement. Instead, he purchased 5,000 acres and in 1897 opened a nine-hole golf course. The following year he expanded the course to eighteen holes. From these modest beginnings would evolve one of the nation's best-known and most successful golf resorts.

Modern tennis also was introduced to the state during this period. Like golf, tennis was considered by many to be a "sissified" sport and was largely confined to polite society, although it became popular on college campuses before golf did. Many of the early golf courses and country clubs offered some type of tennis facility to its membership. The North Carolina Lawn Tennis Association, formed in Raleigh in 1890, began to make some attempts to spread the appeal of the sport.

Of course, the upper class did not look solely to new sports like golf and tennis for its recreation. Horse racing maintained some hold on the state's aristocracy. Breeding, training, and racing fine thoroughbreds remained a way of validating membership in a polite and discriminating society. Another antebellum sport that maintained popularity among the aristocracy was hunting. The appeal of sport hunting was as strong for the New South captains of industry as it had been for their antebellum plantation counterparts. By the end of the century the state was dotted with such exclusive hunting preserves as the 125,000-acre Biltmore estate near Asheville, the 19,000-acre Shocco Game Association in Warren County, and the 15,000-acre Mebane Hunting Lodge in Rockingham County. The Currituck Shooting Club, the Pine Island Club, the Monkey Island Club, the Narrows Island Club, and the Swan Island Club were some of the numerous duck-hunting facilities located in the eastern part of the state.

The postwar development of the nationwide rail system enabled wealthy sport hunters from outside North Carolina to frequent these hunting establishments. The Currituck Shooting Club, for example, received national publicity in such magazines as *Outing* and *Field and Stream* and was largely patronized by northerners. Resorts actively

"Field trials of sporting dogs at High Point, North Carolina," ca. 1886. Engraving from *Harper's Weekly*, XXXI (January 8, 1887), 20.

courted northern patronage. The Moore County community of Southern Pines held a "Week of Sport" during which, according to an 1891 issue of *Harper's Weekly*, "The New Englanders and Northerners assimilated easily with the native farmers. . . . In that week foxes, rabbits, quail, and 'possums are hunted and their lives made miserable or ended abruptly."

Although North Carolina sports remained largely a male preserve during this period, women did begin to make some inroads. The prevalent view remained that sports were inappropriate and unwomanly for females, too strenuous and demanding on delicate constitutions, and dangerous to a woman's reproductive capacity. Some women resisted these stereotypes, however. Most advances made during this period resulted from the activities of educated, upper-class women who possessed both some leisure time and the inclination to use it in new ways. Women participated in such "refined" sports as gymnastics, tennis, and croquet. Nonetheless, these activities were unstructured and generally noncompetitive. There was little opportunity for women to take part in intercollegiate athletics or formal team sports.

The late nineteenth-century sport most closely associated with emerging female freedom was bicycling. As in other parts of the United States, the Tar Heel State was infatuated with the bicycle in the last two decades of the nineteenth century. Bicycle clubs were common in North Carolina cities by the 1890s, and some communities even had races. By the 1890s the sport was feverishly contested at the State Fair. Although men were as enthusiastic about the bicycle as women, it was the latter who were most affected by its popularity. The long skirts that had hindered women's participation in athletics were so obviously dangerous on a bicycle that they were replaced by the less-confining outfit named for its founder, Amelia Bloomer. The clothing known as bloomers and those who wore them became symbolic of newly emergent female athletic capabilities.

During one of North Carolina's "Colored State Fairs" of the 1870s and 1880s, an artist recorded this view of a "walking-match between Negro pedestrians." Engraving from *Frank Leslie's Illustrated Newspaper,* December 6, 1879.

For North Carolina's black population, sports in this period were as segregated as other aspects of the state's society. Such country club activities as horse racing, golf, and tennis were outside the experience of Tar Heel blacks. The most popular formal sport among blacks was baseball, further evidence of that sport's ability to cross all lines. As was common generally, black baseball teams were organized much like a social club. Play was spirited but informal, lacking leagues, schedules, champions, and other characteristics of twentieth-century baseball. Hunting and fishing continued to maintain a strong hold on black communities, although once again in a very informal way. Beginning in 1879, the North Carolina Industrial Association hosted a "Colored State Fair" in the capital city of Raleigh. This fair was severely handicapped by financial constraints and, unlike its white counterpart, was not an important venue for sports.

IV: 1900-1918

Spectator sports in North Carolina increased in popularity and sophistication during the early years of the twentieth century. Despite some setbacks and false starts, Tar Heel sports enthusiasts were able to watch more sports during this period—and what they watched increasingly took on the characteristics of modern sports. A number of sports benefited from an increase in organizational complexity as bureaucracies continued to become more prevalent. Continued improvements in transportation and communication enabled the state's sporting scene to become part of a larger national context; this in turn resulted in standardized rules and playing conditions, increased attention to statistics and records, and a chance for the better North Carolina athletes, at least occasionally, to compete on a regional or national basis. Newspapers gave increased coverage to local, national, and international sports. Most of the larger dailies had formal sports sections by the advent of World War I.

Much of this development can be attributed to two factors: increased urbanization and the increased popularity of sports on college campuses. At the beginning of the twentieth century less than 10 percent of North Carolina's population of 1.8 million was classified as urban. A combination of hard times on the farm and the increasing social and economic appeal of the city fueled a movement from farm to city that saw the state's urban population increase to almost a half-million in 1920, nearly 20 percent of the state's total population. Much of this increase came in the piedmont, although the mountain city of Asheville doubled its population during this twenty-year period. During the same time Winston-Salem's population increased from 13,000 to 48,000, while Charlotte's increased from 18,000 to 46,000. Durham's population tripled, while that of Raleigh, Greensboro, Fayetteville, and Goldsboro doubled.

These newly burgeoning cities provided a number of crucial factors necessary for the development of spectator sports, including population density, facilities, media attention, and occasionally fierce interurban rivalries. Perhaps most importantly, the cities provided a growing class of desk-bound business and professional people with the inclination, leisure time, and financial resources to patronize sports.

Educators increasingly came to feel that college students had valid recreational needs. Although the exact form that college athletics would take was the subject of some debate, particularly heated where football was concerned, there existed a general consensus that college athletics taught valuable lessons such as self-reliance, honor, courage, and "pluck." College athletics also provided a much-needed release for spectators, promoted school spirit, and increasingly served as a focus for alumni interest and support.

During the early years of the twentieth century, professional baseball solidified its position as America's leading spectator sport, in the process becoming increasingly associated with urban areas. The American League claimed major league status in 1901, joining the National League at that exalted level. Following a brief war the two leagues declared a truce, and the national pastime entered a new era of prosperity. The first World Series was played in 1903 and, following a year's absence, returned in 1905 to become the nation's foremost sporting event. In the fall of 1901 the National Association of Professional Baseball Leagues was formed, bringing the minor leagues under the umbrella of organized baseball. The National Association established a classification system for minor leagues, set salary limits and team roster limits, and created reserve rights in which teams would be compensated for losing players to higher leagues. The National Association would prove vital for the survival and eventual expansion of minor league baseball.

Professional baseball in North Carolina during this period, as in the rest of the South, meant minor league baseball. Minor league ball became firmly entrenched in the state by the end of the new century's first decade, but not before several disappointing false starts. In 1901, 1902, and 1905 leagues were formed amid hoopla and high hopes, only to fold before completing their season. In 1901 Raleigh and Wilmington, along with the Virginia cities of Newport News, Norfolk, Portsmouth, and Richmond, fielded teams in the Virginia-North Carolina League. At midseason the troubled league moved the Newport News and Portsmouth franchises to Tarboro and Charlotte respectively. Shortly thereafter the two remaining Virginia clubs folded, leaving a four-team North Carolina league that lasted until the middle of August. The following year the North Carolina State League, with teams in Charlotte, Durham, Greensboro, New Bern, Raleigh, and Wilmington, became the first Tar Heel league to operate under the new National Association rules. Despite this apparent advantage, the league also folded prematurely. After a two-year hiatus, league ball returned in 1905 in a second, more modest Virginia-North Carolina League. Teams were established in Charlotte, Greensboro, Salisbury-Spencer (later moved to Winston), and Danville, Virginia. This league was no more successful than its predecessors and disbanded early.

These three leagues suffered from a variety of ills, including inadequate financing, inexperienced administration and management, poor umpiring, and an inadequate number of fans. Nevertheless, such young men as Durham attorney William G. Bramham and Charlotte merchant J. H. Wearn learned valuable administrative lessons that would serve them well in their subsequent careers as presidents of minor leagues.

The next attempts to make league ball workable came in 1908 when not one but two leagues answered the call. The Eastern Carolina Baseball League was made up of teams in Goldsboro, Kinston, New Bern, Raleigh, Wilmington, and Wilson. To the west the Carolina Association had teams in Charlotte, Greensboro, Winston, and the South Carolina cities of Anderson, Greenville, and Spartanburg. These new leagues required a firmer adherence to the National Association's salary limit, stronger central control, and a requirement that teams post bond to demonstrate fiscal responsibility. Both of these leagues successfully completed an entire season, although the Eastern League did lose Kinston and New Bern before the end of the campaign.

The Carolina Association, under the enthusiastic leadership of league president J. H. Wearn, a Charlotte businessman, played through the 1912 season without a single franchise shift. The Eastern Carolina Association was more fluid, adding Fayetteville and Rocky Mount and losing Goldsboro and Wilmington. In the mountains Asheville played in the Appalachian League in 1911 and 1912, the only North Carolina team in that association. In 1913 the strongest cities from these three leagues formed the North Carolina State League, which consisted of Asheville, Charlotte, Durham, Greensboro, Raleigh, and Winston-Salem.

These North Carolina leagues were fairly unremarkable components of organized baseball. Few of their players made the big leagues, and fewer still are remembered today. Some had spectacular seasons, however, including several pitchers who challenged the magic thirty-win barrier. In 1911 J. E. Swindell of Winston's Carolina Association team won 29 games against only 8 losses and struck out 250 batters. In 1914 Carl Ray of Winston-Salem, then in the North Carolina Association, won 28, lost 15, and struck out 315. The following year Elmer Myers of Raleigh won 29 games and lost 10 in the North Carolina League.

Ironically, the best-known minor league player in the Tar Heel State during this period was a player who compiled fairly mediocre statistics. In 1909 a young Indian from Pennsylvania joined the Rocky Mount team in the Eastern Carolina Association. As a pitcher and first baseman he won 9 games, lost 10, and batted .253. The following year, with Rocky Mount out of the league, he played for the Fayetteville team. The player was Jim Thorpe, the greatest athlete of his time and winner of the decathlon in the 1912 Olympics. When news of Thorpe's professional career in North Carolina surfaced, he was forced to relinquish his gold medal and his amateur status.

Of course, baseball in the state was not confined only to formal minor league ball. Throughout North Carolina, baseball continued to be enormously popular, both as a spectator and participant sport. Semiprofessional, amateur, and school teams existed in every community. Vacant lots, schoolyards, and fields were filled with baseball players from the first days of spring to the chill of autumn. The increased attention paid to the national pastime by local newspapers enabled the true fan to follow the big leagues, including the increasingly large numbers of North Carolinians playing in the big cities. Several of these men were players of consequence. Durham native George (Possum) Whitted played in more than 1,000 games in a National League career running from 1912 to 1922; his career batting average was .270. Clinton's Rube Benton pitched for three National League teams from 1910 until 1925, winning 156 games and losing 145. George Suggs of Kinston compiled a big league won-lost record of 100-88, while Ernie Shore of East Bend won 65 and lost 42. Shore, who after retiring from baseball served for many years as sheriff of Forsyth County, figured prominently in one of baseball's most famous games. On June 23, 1917, Boston Red Sox pitcher Babe Ruth, not yet a famous Yankee outfielder, started against the Washington Senators. Ruth walked the lead-off batter, all the while arguing vociferously with the umpire. Ruth was ejected after giving up this walk and was relieved by Shore. The base runner was thrown out attempting to steal, whereupon Shore proceeded to retire the next twenty-six batters. Following some debate by league officials, Shore was credited with a perfect game, thereby becoming the only pitcher in major league history to pitch a no-hitter in relief.

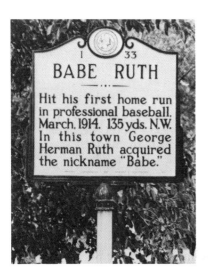

This North Carolina highway historical marker commemorates Babe Ruth's first home run in professional baseball, which took place in Fayetteville in March, 1914. Ruth, then noted more for his talents as a pitcher than as a hitter, acquired the nickname Babe while playing in the North Carolina town. Photograph from the files of the Division of Archives and History.

Baseball retained its popularity on the state's college campuses. Virtually every school had a team, and some heated rivalries developed. A particularly strong rivalry existed between North Carolina A&M and Wake Forest, which were located only a few miles apart in Wake County. Games were routinely scheduled against northern schools. The University of North Carolina, for example, played against such schools as Amherst, Cornell, Lehigh, Princeton, St. John's, Yale, and the United States Naval Academy. A 1910 game between Trinity and the University of Delaware, won by the former, 1-0, attracted statewide attention. The sport was particularly popular and successful at Trinity College, where the football ban continued. One Trinity pitcher, Arthur Bradsher, became known as the "King of the Southern Diamond" in 1905, while three years later Bob Gantt hurled three no-hitters in leading the school to a record of 20 wins, 4 losses, and 1 tie. The 1908 Trinity team has been touted as the best state college team of the early twentieth century, a claim that could easily be challenged by the 1910 A&M team, which won 18 of 19 games.

Organized baseball was off-limits to blacks in this period. Major League baseball had erected an unwritten but firm ban against blacks, and the Negro Leagues were not formed until after World War I. For this reason the state's black colleges were hotbeds of baseball. Schools such as Shaw, Biddle Institute, Livingstone, St. Augustine's, and North Carolina A&T played not only each other but also other black schools from across the nation. The segregated society of the time prevented the black schools from competing against their white counterparts.

Despite its popularity, college baseball had two major problems. The academic calendar, and thus the college season, ended in May, just when serious baseball was ready to heat up. More importantly, the development of minor league ball in the state gave fans access to a higher quality of ball than that played by the students. In the first decade of the century, college teams regularly played exhibition games against minor league teams and just as regularly lost, despite the fact that these games, usually played in April, came during the peak of the college season and were preseason games for the pros. Once it became apparent that the college game was not up to the level of minor league ball, the former lost some of its luster. This was not a problem for football, however, and the younger sport used this opening to challenge and eventually overtake baseball as the most popular campus game.

College football still had its share of critics, however. The problem of violence continued unabated in the early years of the century. After a dozen deaths in 1902, the *Journal of the American Medical Association* called for the abolition of the game, a cry that increased in intensity after the 1904 season saw twenty-one fatalities. In October, 1905, President Theodore Roosevelt met with officials from Harvard, Yale, and Princeton in an attempt to place controls on the game. With Roosevelt's prodding in mind, the leading football schools made a number of crucial rules changes prior to the 1906 season, the most important of which were the legalization of the forward pass and a reduction in the length of games from ninety minutes to sixty minutes. The newly legalized forward pass became increasingly prevalent just before the war. With these changes the game opened up, became safer, and slowly gained respectability.

In North Carolina many continued to question the proper place of football on the college campus. Despite frequent appeals by students, the football ban continued at Trinity. Wake Forest reinstituted football in 1908 but paid a competitive price for its thirteen-year absence at that school. The 1908 team won only one of five games and was followed by a long string of losing teams, the worst of which was the 1913 aggregation, which was outscored on the season by 30 points to 200 points on the way to an 0-8 mark. Indeed, Wake's first winning season in the twentieth century didn't come until 1923. Other sectarian schools, such as Davidson, Elon, and Guilford, allowed football only under strict limits.

This largely left the field open for the two large state-supported schools, UNC and A&M. UNC had winning seasons more often than not. The most successful was the 1914 team, which won its first ten games before bowing to the University of Virginia in its finale, 20-3. This game was played before 15,000 fans in Richmond, evidence of the rapidly developing popularity of college football. Other successful teams included those of 1901 (7-2), 1902 (5-1-3), and 1911 (6-1-1). UNC's opponents consisted largely of colleges located in North Carolina and the South but included such eastern powers as Pennsylvania, the Naval Academy, Princeton, and Harvard. The university's biggest rivalry was with the University of Virginia, not its in-state rival A&M. UNC and A&M rarely played during this period. Following a scoreless tie in 1905—the third consecutive tie between the two schools—the series was canceled because of A&M's insistence on allowing a postgraduate student to play on the team. The resulting eligibility dispute kept the two rivals apart until after the Great War.

A&M found other opponents, of course, and developed a particularly strong rivalry with Virginia's fellow land-grant college, Virginia Polytechnic Institute. The best A&M teams were those from 1907 through 1910, which compiled successive records of 6-0-1, 6-1, 6-1, and 4-0-2. The 1913 team was 6-1 and the 1917 team 6-2-1. Not every A&M team reached such lofty heights, of course. A nadir of sorts came in 1918 when the team, weakened by the loss of its best players to the war effort and ravaged by the Spanish influenza epidemic, made an ill-advised journey to Atlanta to play powerful Georgia Tech. The Golden Tornadoes, coached by the legendary John Heisman, drubbed A&M 128-0 in a game mercifully stopped early in the fourth quarter.

The state's black colleges also fielded football teams. Shaw, Livingstone, Biddle Institute, A&T, and others developed healthy rivalries not only with other in-state institutions but also with out-of-state schools such as Virginia Union, Morehouse, Howard, and South Carolina State. The North Carolina teams held their own, as demonstrated by Livingstone's undefeated teams in 1913 and 1915.

Although baseball and football dominated campus sports, there were other options. Basketball was played but was far from the popular sport it would later become. It was regarded as little more than a winter diversion between the outdoor activities of football and baseball. Unlike most sports, which evolved over a period of time, basketball was invented. In 1891 a Springfield, Massachusetts, YMCA director named James Naismith came up with the sport in an attempt to find an indoor activity that would interest his students through the harsh New England winter. North Carolina's YMCAs were points of entry for basketball in the Tar Heel State.

The first schools to play intercollegiate basketball in North Carolina were Wake Forest, Guilford, and Trinity. The first college game apparently was a February 6, 1906, contest between Wake Forest and Guilford, won by the latter 26-19. Later that winter Wake Forest played and won two games against Trinity. Davidson in 1908, the University of North Carolina in 1911, A&M in 1911, Elon in 1912, and Livingstone in 1917 were among the numerous North Carolina colleges to begin playing college basketball prior to World War I.

The first dominant basketball figure in the state was Wake Forest coach Richard Crozier, who compiled a record of 95 wins and 46 losses while directing his team from 1906 through 1917. The 1916 Wake Forest team won 16 of 18 games, including an 89-8 thumping of Guilford. The 1917 Trinity team was 20-4 and was probably the first team in the state to win twenty games in a single season. Schools generally did not adhere to the kind of intersectional schedules played by their football and baseball counterparts. For example, Trinity's schedule during this period included such opponents as Littleton High School, the Statesville Athletic Club, Trinity Park (a high school), and the Winston, Charlotte, and Durham YMCAs. Indeed, local Y's were frequent opponents for college teams and even won some games from the collegians.

Track and field and tennis were also popular sports on many campuses. With football and baseball becoming increasingly specialized, track and field especially was viewed as a sport in which the average student could participate. Gymnastics was recognized as beneficial for all students, particularly females, whose participation in athletics continued to be circumscribed by the social mores of the time, which characterized competition between women as unbecoming and frivolous.

Golf, tennis, horse racing and sport hunting remained popular sports with the upper class. Of these, only sport hunting was not viewed as the particular province of the elite during this period. Of course, only the well-to-do had access to the restricted hunting clubs that became

Members of the 1900 basketball team at North Carolina State Normal and Industrial College, forerunner of the University of North Carolina at Greensboro. Photograph courtesy UNC-G.

increasingly popular throughout the state. The growth of urbanization and industrialization led to an increased interest in returning to the wild. For the first time the state's hunters, whether they were captains of industry or humble farmers, became subject to major restrictions on hunting, particularly a 1903 law that protected game birds and established regulations for hunting. These rules were originally regulated by the Audubon Society. North Carolina hunters resisted attempts to regulate hunting. They protested the establishment of hunting and fishing licenses so vociferously that the licenses were at first given free to residents of the state but sold to outsiders.

Horse racing continued its slow, steady decline. Although both trotting and flat racing remained regular components of the State Fair and county fairs, the racing scene was stymied by the refusal of the state to allow the kind of formalized race betting that became the norm in major horse-racing states. Horse racing's distant cousin, cockfighting, was officially banned in the early part of the century, although it continued to attract enthusiastic devotees throughout the state, particularly in rural regions.

Golf and tennis, particularly the former, became popular mainstays of the country club set. Among North Carolina's new golf courses were the Charlotte Country Club, founded in 1910, the Greensboro Country Club (1911), and the Raleigh Country Club (1911). The center of golf in the

An early golf tournament at a country club in Pinehurst, about 1912. Note the square configuration of the putting surface. From picture postcard in the possession of Stephen E. Massengill, Raleigh.

state, however, was the Sandhills region, particularly Pinehurst, where Richard Tufts's resort was gaining national fame and national visitors. Scotsman Donald Ross arrived at Pinehurst in 1900. Ross, one of the country's foremost golf course designers, constructed the famous Pinehurst Course No. 2, which was finished in 1907. In 1901 Pinehurst hosted the first annual North and South Amateur Tournament, which is still a highly regarded annual event. In 1903 a North and South professional event was inaugurated. The first winner of this event was Donald Ross. More important, perhaps, was the establishment in 1903 of the North and South Women's Amateur, the first serious athletic competition for women in North Carolina. Mrs. M. D. Patterson, a New Jersey native, won three of the first four women's tournaments. Tennis, although a popular pastime in some quarters, did not develop at a pace comparable to golf.

Not everyone could belong to a country club, of course. An increasingly large number of desk-bound urban workers took advantage of small but growing recreational opportunities. The YMCA and YWCA, introduced to the state in the nineteenth century, gained in popularity throughout the early years of the twentieth century and offered a variety of sporting, educational, and social opportunities. The state's urban areas, dominated to a large extent by the business hierarchy, came late to the idea of public recreation. Public recreational facilities such as Latta Park in Charlotte, Pullen Park and Bloomsbury Park in Raleigh, and Fisher Park in Greensboro offered city residents some relief from urban anxieties. Many of these parks were located in or near the newly emerging suburban living areas. The average Tar Heel had little access to these facilities, however, and the general physical fitness of the state's citizenry was not impressive. State leaders were appalled by the high number of North Carolinians deemed physically unfit for duty during World War I. In spite of some advances, sports in early twentieth-century North Carolina remained very much the province of an educated, urban professional class.

V: 1918-1945

After World War I American sports entered a period sports historian Benjamin Rader has termed the Age of the Spectator. Urbanization, increased leisure time, and the development of radio combined with a postwar desire for escapism, adventure, and entertainment to turn sports stars, actors, and entertainers into household words and lead spectator sports to new heights of popularity. Athletes such as Babe Ruth, Red Grange, Jack Dempsey, Knute Rockne, Bill Tilden, Walter Hagen, and Bobby Jones became national heroes and in many cases were viewed as role models for America's impressionable youth. By the end of the 1920s big-time spectator sports had become such a fundamental part of the American landscape that they were able to survive the Great Depression, although not without some retrenchment.

Sports also increased in popularity in North Carolina during the 1920s. Minor league baseball in the state was led by the highly successful Piedmont League, founded in 1920. Likewise, the Southern Conference, created in 1921, gave increased attention to college athletics in the state. Football, although not above criticism, continued to solidify its hold as the dominant sport on college campuses, with basketball gaining in popularity in the academic setting. Tennis, track and field, and other sports rounded out the college experience. Even boxing became a popular college sport for a brief period in the 1930s. Away from academia, a proliferation of golf courses throughout the state was evidence of the rising appeal of a sport that was becoming increasingly associated with North Carolina.

Baseball remained the preferred sport for most Tar Heels. In *Southerners: Portrait of a People* newsman Charles Kuralt, who was reared in several North Carolina communities, reminisced: "Wherever you lived, no matter what school you went to or what you did for a living, there was a baseball team playing nearby. The smell of a catcher's mitt was universal, as were the crack of a good hit, the smell of a hot dog, the dust on your britches." It was not uncommon for a given community to have a professional minor league team, a college team or two, high school teams, semiprofessional and amateur nines, church leagues, textile leagues, and informal sandlot games occupying every available vacant lot.

With the nearest major league franchises in the distant North or Midwest, the numerous minor league teams were the apex of baseball in the state. The dominant figure in Tar Heel minor league ball was Durham attorney William G. Bramham, founder and president of the Piedmont league, president of the South Atlantic, Eastern Carolina, and Virginia leagues, and an active force in the National Association of Professional Baseball Leagues. The Piedmont League had its baptism in 1920 with franchises in Raleigh, Durham, Winston-Salem, Greensboro, High Point, and Danville, Virginia. The league had a shifting membership that eventually included franchises in Asheville, Charlotte, Henderson, Rocky Mount, Salisbury, and Wilmington, in addition to several Virginia cities. It was regarded as one of the better minor leagues of its size and gave Tar Heel baseball fans a high quality of ball.

The league featured such stars as Lloyd Smith, who batted .404 for Greensboro in 1921; Carr Smith, who batted .418 for Raleigh two years later; and High Point's Cliff Bolton, who batted .403 in 1928. The unquestioned star of the circuit, however, was a hard-hitting High Point slugger named Dan Boone, who led the league in batting four times, in home runs twice, and in runs batted in twice from 1926 through 1930. Boone won the triple crown in 1928 with a .419 batting average, 38 home runs, and 131 rbi's. Although the Smiths, Bolton, and Boone never achieved major league stardom, the Piedmont League did feature a number of future top-level big leaguers, including Hank Greenberg (Raleigh), Johnny Mize (Greensboro), Charles Grimm (Durham), Johnny Vander Meer (Durham), Phil Rizzuto (Norfolk), Johnny Pesky (Rocky Mount), Frank McCormick (Durham), and Yogi Berra (Norfolk).

Other minor leagues were represented by North Carolina cities. Charlotte and Asheville were members of the Southern League prior to joining the Piedmont League. Rocky Mount and Wilson were members of the Virginia League in the 1920s, while the Bi-State League, founded in 1934, had franchises in both North Carolina and Virginia. The Coastal Plains League existed as a semipro organization for years before joining the National Association in 1937. A geographically compact league, it boasted teams in Ayden, Goldsboro, Greenville, Kinston, New Bern, Snow Hill, Tarboro, and Williamston. Also in 1937 the North Carolina State League was revived, with teams in such relatively small western piedmont communities as Shelby, Lexington, Mooresville, and Salisbury.

The Great Depression hit minor league baseball hard, in North Carolina and elsewhere. By 1932 only a handful of minor leagues were still operating. In December of that year Durham's William G. Bramham was elected president of the National Association. Bramham was a firm believer in fiscal integrity and a firm advocate of stronger central control. Under his leadership and in light of the threat posed by the Depression, minor league baseball became more professional and eventually gained back its losses. Minor league ball in North Carolina during the 1930s

46

benefited from additional changes. Lights made night baseball possible, while the gradual decline of blue laws enabled the minor leagues to play on Sundays. These changes made it easier for working men and women to attend games and become supporters of the teams.

North Carolina gained a well-deserved reputation during this period as a successful incubator of big league talent. Numerous native Tar Heels excelled on major league diamonds. The Ferrell brothers, reared in Greensboro, are among the best-known baseball siblings. Older brother Rick, a catcher, played in nearly 2,000 games in an eighteen-year career, batting .281 and recording 1,692 hits. He is a member of baseball's Hall of Fame. Pitcher Wes Ferrell won 193 games in the majors against only 128 losses, including a no-hitter in 1931 while hurling for the Cleveland Indians. A third brother, George Ferrell, was a longtime minor league star.

Another member of the Hall of Fame is Luke Appling, born in High Point but reared in Georgia. Other North Carolinians to play in the majors included Buddy Lewis of Gastonia, who batted .297 in an eleven-year career with the Washington Senators; Burgess Whitehead of Tarboro, a key member of the St. Louis Cardinals "Gas House Gang" of the 1930s; Taffy Wright of Tabor City, a lifetime .311 hitter; pitcher Johnny Allen of Lenoir, whose 142-75 won-lost record included a 17-4 season for the 1932 world champion New York Yankees in his rookie season and a spectacular 15-1 record for the 1937 Cleveland Indians; Alvin Crowder of Winston-Salem, who won a league-leading 24 games, against 15 losses, for the 1933 American League champion Washington Senators and compiled a lifetime record of 167-115; Max Lanier of Denton, winner of 108 games and an important member of the outstanding St. Louis Cardinal teams of the 1940s; and Tom Zachary of Graham, who won 185 regular season games and 3 World Series games, ran up a 12-0 season in 1929, and who is best remembered for giving up Babe Ruth's famous sixtieth home run in 1927. Zachary's perfect 1929 season remains the major league record for most victories without a loss in a season.

Still conspicuous by their absence from the major leagues were black players, barred from the big time by an unwritten but firm ban. The Negro Leagues offered some opportunity for especially skilled black players. But the absence of an extensive black minor league system comparable to the one supported by "organized baseball" doomed lesser talents to informal, makeshift contests.

One of the premier players in the Negro Leagues was Rocky Mount native Walter (Buck) Leonard, a hard-hitting first baseman dubbed "the black Lou Gehrig." Leonard played for the Baltimore Stars and the Brooklyn Royal Giants but had his best years in the 1930s and early 1940s with the Homestead (Pennsylvania) Grays, where he teamed with Josh Gibson to form the most feared one-two punch in black baseball. Leonard played in the Negro League all-star game twelve times. In 1972 he was

The great standout of baseball's old Negro Leagues, Walter (Buck) Leonard. Photograph courtesy National Baseball Library, Cooperstown, New York.

elected to baseball's Hall of Fame. North Carolina native Charles Taylor was one of the best black managers (he died prematurely in 1922), while Marion native William Greenlee was important as the owner of the Pittsburgh Crawfords in the 1930s.

College football increased in popularity and sophistication throughout the 1920s and survived the difficult 1930s. Radio coverage of games, improved transportation to college sites, and enlarged newspaper and magazine coverage led to increased support among both alumni and fans not otherwise associated with a particular school. New stadiums were built to accommodate the demand, while programs gained new financial stability. National recruiting and intersectional scheduling increasingly came to characterize North Carolina football. There was a dark side to this increased attention, however. Intensive recruiting led to abuses and an overemphasis on football that educators tried, with mixed success, to combat. The 1929 report *American College Athletics*, published by the Carnegie Foundation, focused national attention on the growing problems of reconciling big-time athletics with higher education. Locally, North Carolina colleges were particularly plagued by coaching instability. As alumni groups showed more support for football, they also sought more influence. Schools changed coaches with remarkable rapidity, constantly seeking a miracle worker who could satisfy increasingly strident alumni demands for wins.

The University of North Carolina resumed football after the war years in 1919. In 1921 brothers Bill and Bob Fetzer became co-coaches, an unusual situation that prevailed for five seasons. Two of the Fetzer teams excelled. The 1922 Tar Heels, led by multisport star Angus (Monk) McDonald, won nine games against only a single 18-0 loss at Yale. Highlights of the season were a 62-3 thrashing of Wake Forest and a 20-0 win over Trinity in the first twentieth-century meeting of those two schools. The 1925 UNC team went 7-1-1. The season finale, a hard-fought 3-3 tie against the University of Virginia, was played before an overflow crowd of 16,000 in 2,400-seat-capacity Emerson Field in a game that graphically illustrated the new popularity of college football in the state. Emerson Field was replaced in 1927 by Kenan Field, which featured a one-game crowd of 28,000 in its inaugural season.

Chuck Collins replaced the Fetzers as football coach in 1926. After three mediocre seasons, Collins hit the jackpot in 1929, winning nine games against only a 19-12 loss to the University of Georgia. This extremely deep team scored 346 points, gave up only 60, and became famous as "The Team of a Million Backs." Collins was unable to duplicate this success, however. Depression economics led to a decline in the recruiting budget, which in turn led to Collins's departure after consecutive losing seasons in 1932 and 1933.

Collins was replaced by nationally known Carl Snavely, a proven winner at Bucknell. Snavely immediately turned the program around, going 7-1-2 in 1934 under the leadership of UNC's first football all-American, guard George Barclay. Snavely continued his success in 1935. The Tar Heels won their first eight games and were being touted as a Rose Bowl possibility before their final game, a shocking and disappointing 25-0 loss to Duke. Despite this impressive record, Snavely ran afoul of reform-minded UNC president Frank Porter Graham, whose "Graham Plan," proposed in 1935, would have de-emphasized football in the Southern Conference. After long and acrimonious debate, the proposal failed. The disillusioned Snavely, nonetheless, left for greener pastures after the 1935 season. His replacement, Ray Wolf, continued the program at a high level, posting winning seasons in five of his six seasons and producing all-Americans Andy Bershak and Paul Severin.

Trinity College resumed football in 1920 following an absence of a quarter-century. The team had some success in the early 1920s but against a low level of competition. In 1924 Trinity became Duke University. As competition toughened, Duke's record deteriorated. Duke President William Preston Few and other members of the school hierarchy felt that a nationally prominent football program could help publicize the school. Trinity/Duke ran through seven coaches in the 1920s before meeting with success. Duke Stadium was completed in 1929, helping make the school financially competitive with any in the state.

In 1931 Duke hired Wallace Wade as head football coach to replace James DeHart. (Ironically, DeHart was let go following an 8-1-2 season, the only winning season of his five-year tenure.) Wade came from the University of Alabama, where he had coached three Rose Bowl teams. He quickly turned his new school into a national power. In 1933 Duke, led by lineman Fred Crawford, the state's first football all-American, won its first nine games before a controversial 6-0 loss to Georgia Tech knocked the Blue Devils out of the Rose Bowl. Wade followed this with four consecutive winning seasons. Most gratifying to Blue Devil fans were four wins in five years over UNC, in what was becoming one of the South's fiercest rivalries.

Wade's best-known team was the famous "Iron Duke" team of 1938. Led by all-Americans Dan Hill and Eric Tipton and future all-American George McAfee, Duke not only won its first nine games but did so without allowing the opposition to score a single point. The regular season ended with a dramatic 7-0 victory over perennial national power Pittsburgh that propelled the undefeated and unscored-on Blue Devils into the Rose Bowl against Southern California. Duke carried a precarious 3-0 lead into the game's final minute before a Southern Cal touchdown handed the Blue Devils a heartbreaking 7-3 defeat.

Duke regrouped with 8-1 and 7-2 seasons in 1939 and 1940. The 1941 eleven won all nine of its regular-season games to earn another trip to the Rose Bowl, scheduled for January 1, 1942. Following the Japanese attack on Pearl Harbor the game was hastily rescheduled for Durham and Duke Stadium. In the most famous football game ever played in North

Wallace Wade, head football coach at Duke University from 1931 to 1941, turned the Blue Devils into a national power, produced the fabled "Iron Duke" team of 1938, and led his 1941 team to the 1942 Rose Bowl, played in Durham for reasons of national security. Following active service in World War II, he also coached the Duke football squad from 1946 through 1950. Photograph courtesy Duke Sports Information, Durham.

Carolina, Duke suffered another close loss, 20-16, to Oregon State. Shortly afterward, Wade received a commission as a major in the United States Army. In eleven seasons he had compiled a record at Duke of 85-19-3. Wade and six of his prewar players—Hill, Tipton, McAfee, Clarence (Ace) Parker, Fred Crawford, and Steve Lach—are members of the National Football Foundation College Football Hall of Fame. New coach Eddie Cameron continued to produce winning teams during the war years and coached the Blue Devils to a Sugar Bowl victory over Alabama at the conclusion of the 1944 season.

In addition to UNC and Duke, the other three members of the so-called "Big Five" were North Carolina State, Wake Forest, and Davidson. All three had a difficult time competing with the Snavelys and the Wades of the football world. North Carolina State was a virtual coaching grave-yard. The Wolfpack ran through eight coaches in the interwar period and compiled only six winning seasons from 1919 through 1941. Alumni pressure was a constant thorn in the side of the school administration and led to the departure of several coaches. This dismal trend was briefly but brilliantly interrupted in a spectacular 1927 season. Coached by Gus Tebell and led by all-American back Jack McDowall, State won nine games and lost one—to Furman. Only two years later, however, State was 1-8 and coach Tebell was gone. The 1930s were notable only for a 6-1-2 season in 1932.

Wake Forest was briefly successful in the middle 1920s under the tutelage of coach Hank Garrity. His three-year record of 19-7-1 was headlined by the 1924 team, which defeated Duke, Elon, Guilford, North Carolina State, and UNC en route to a 7-2 season. After Garrity left, the program declined, reaching a nadir in an 0-5-1 1933 season. In 1937 Douglas Clyde (Peahead) Walker became head coach at Wake Forest and slowly turned the program around. Wake Forest went 7-3 in both 1939 and 1940.

Davidson football reached a peak under the coaching of Monk Younger in the middle 1920s. In 1924, 1925, and 1926 Davidson put together successive records of 6-2-1, 6-3-1, and 7-2-1. The Wildcats won less often in the 1930s, although halfback Johnny Mackorell won some all-American acclaim in 1934.

The smaller colleges in the state also had their followers. The North State League featured competition among Elon, Appalachian State Teachers College (later University), Catawba, Guilford, Lenoir Rhyne, and other schools. Appalachian State had particularly good teams in the middle 1930s under coaches Kidd Brewer and Flucie Stewart, losing only four times from 1936 through 1939. Catawba's 8-0-1 1930 season and 9-1 1935 season headlined that school's program, while Elon's 7-1 season in 1937 is worthy of mention.

The state's black colleges also developed some fierce rivalries during this period. North Carolina A&T lost more games than it won but had a

7-0 season in 1927 and a 7-1 season in 1934. North Carolina College (later North Carolina Central University) won its first Central Intercollegiate Athletic Association (CIAA) championship with a 6-1-1 record in 1941. Johnson C. Smith University had several outstanding teams in the late 1920s led by all-star tackle Johnny Bogle and in the late 1930s and early 1940s under the leadership of end Jack Brayboy and halfback Kenneth Powell.

White college football players during this period had an option not available to players of an earlier era. The National Football League, although not yet a serious rival to professional baseball, became a viable part of the American sports scene in the 1930s. Numerous players with North Carolina connections were professional players in the 1930s and 1940s, although few achieved stardom. The best known were former Duke stars Ace Parker and George McAfee. Parker, who also played major league baseball, played pro football from 1937 until 1946, with a break for military service during World War II. Parker was named the league's Most Valuable Player in 1940, the same year he led the NFL in interceptions. George McAfee was a standout halfback and feared punt returner for the fabled "Monsters of the Midway," the Chicago Bears. McAfee played on three NFL championship teams. Both Parker and McAfee are members of the Pro Football Hall of Fame. There was even professional football, of a sort, in the state in the 1930s. The Charlotte Clippers played in the minor Southern League and Dixie League in the late 1930s and early 1940s, while Durham, Greensboro, and Winston-Salem made brief attempts at minor league pro football in the 1930s.

Clarence (Ace) Parker, who played football at Duke in the mid-1930s, played professionally from 1937 to 1946, was named the National Football League's Most Valuable Player in 1940, and is a member of the Pro Football Hall of Fame. He also had a brief career as a major league baseball player. Photograph courtesy Duke University; supplied by the North Carolina Sports Hall of Fame, Raleigh.

Basketball gradually increased in popularity but still remained largely a sport to fill the calendar between football and baseball. It became more associated with colleges and high schools in the interwar period and less associated with the YMCA. A few teams and players from the Tar Heel State attained some renown in basketball. As in football, most attention in the state went to the Big Five.

The University of North Carolina had the state's premier basketball program for most of the 1920s and 1930s, including a streak of eighteen consecutive winning seasons. UNC won four of the first six Southern Conference tournaments (1922, 1924, 1925, and 1926) and later won tournaments in 1935, 1936, and 1940. The 1923 Tar Heels were 15-1, losing only in the tournament. They followed that with a perfect 26-0 mark in 1924 and were hailed in some circles as the unofficial national champions. The 1930s were highlighted by a 23-2 season in 1935 and a 21-4 season in 1936. All-American George Glamack led the Tar Heels to consecutive records of 23-3 and 19-9 in 1940 and 1941. In the latter season he was named Helms Foundation National Player of the Year. The Tar Heels made their first appearance in the NCAA tournament in 1941.

The North Carolina State basketball program relied heavily on football players, with mixed success. Football coach Gus Tebell also coached the basketball team, compiling a 78-35 record from 1925 through 1930. Nevertheless, his football failings led to his dismissal from both posts, clear illustration of the relative importance of the two sports in this period. His successor, Doc Sermon, coached for ten years and won 111 games against only 74 losses. Highlights for North Carolina State included a 19-3 record in 1926, an upset Southern Conference tournament championship in 1929, and a 15-4 record in 1936.

Trinity/Duke employed six coaches from 1919 through 1928, with generally poor results. The program turned around under Eddie Cameron, who took over in the 1928-1929 season. Cameron coached fourteen seasons for the Blue Devils, winning 226 games against only 99 losses and suffering only one losing season. Duke won the Southern Conference tournament in 1938, 1941, and 1942. Future major league baseball star Bill Werber won basketball all-American honors for Duke in 1930, and Bill Mock followed ten years later. Duke Indoor Stadium, later named Cameron Indoor Stadium, was opened in 1940, giving Duke the largest such facility in the Carolinas.

Wake Forest's basketball program was competitive for much of the 1920s, including a 22-3 record in 1927 under coach James Baldwin. After 1927, however, the program endured nine consecutive losing seasons. The program stabilized in the late 1930s under the tutelage of Murray Greason. Wake Forest joined the Southern Conference in the fall of 1936. In 1939, under the leadership of Jim Waller, Wake Forest went 18-6 and played in the inaugural NCAA tournament, losing to Ohio State in the opener.

At Davidson Monk Younger also doubled as football and basketball coach in the mid- to late 1920s. His best basketball season was 18-6 in 1925. In the autumn of 1936 Davidson also joined the Southern Conference. The Wildcats were 19-10 in 1939 under Norman Shepard.

In the 1930s Guilford, Elon, Catawba, High Point, Lenoir Rhyne, Atlantic Christian, and Appalachian State played basketball in the Carolinas Conference. This association was the focus of white, small-college basketball in the state. Appalachian sent teams to the National Association of Intercollegiate Athletics (NAIA) championship tournament in 1940, 1941, and 1943, while Catawba finished as NAIA runner-up in 1945. Virgil Yow, the best-known North Carolina small-college coach of the period, directed High Point College's basketball teams. His best player was High Point native Richard Broadus Culler, a four-time all-conference player and 1936 NAIA all-American, who later played major league baseball.

In 1936 John McLendon arrived at North Carolina A&T from the Midwest. McLendon, who in 1961 became the first black to be a head coach in any pro sport, coached a high-scoring aggregation that dominated black college basketball in the state through the 1940s.

Golf continued to gain adherents in North Carolina throughout the 1920s and 1930s. By 1938 the state boasted more than eighty golf courses, a third of which were public facilities. Pinehurst remained the best-known golf resort in the state and one of the best known in the country. Countless golfers traveled to Pinehurst, particularly in the winter, to play the famed No. 2 course. During this period Pinehurst hosted numerous professional and amateur tournaments of local, state, and national significance. In 1929, for example, some sixteen tournaments were held at the Moore County resort. Pinehurst No. 2 hosted the 1936 Professional Golf Association championship, won by Denny Shute. Nevertheless, the various North and South tournaments, both professional and amateur, continued to head Pinehurst's annual schedule.

Pinehurst did have rivals for golfing supremacy in the state. The Carolina Country Club in Raleigh, Winston-Salem's Tanglewood, Greensboro's Starmount Forest, Durham's Hope Valley, and Myers Park Country Club in Charlotte were among the many championship courses that attracted the attention of the golfing populace. Greensboro, Charlotte, Durham, and Asheville all hosted professional golf tournaments in the 1940s. The Greater Greensboro Open (GGO), destined to become the most memo-rable Carolina golf tournament, had its debut in 1938.

These tournaments brought golf's leading lights to the Tar Heel State and enabled North Carolina golf fans to see a high quality of play. For example, Sam Snead won the inaugural GGO. Ben Hogan won the GGO in 1940, and Byron Nelson did so in 1942 and 1945. Indeed, Hogan won three tournaments in the state in 1940, a feat duplicated by Nelson in 1945. Several North Carolinians competed successfully at this high level.

In 1936 Tony Manero, club pro at Greensboro's Sedgefield Country Club, won the United States Open. Clayton Heafner, Johnny Bulla, Skip Alexander, Al Smith, and Johnny Palmer were among other North Carolinians on the pro tour in the 1930s and 1940s.

Although there was no professional golf tour for women prior to World War II, women were seen in increasing numbers on golf courses and in amateur tournaments. Chapel Hill's Estelle Lawson Page was the dominant player in the Carolinas and one of the outstanding women golfers in the world. In a distinguished career she won the 1937 national championship, seven North and South Amateur championships between 1935 and 1945, and numerous other titles.

During the 1930s and 1940s Estelle Lawson Page of Chapel Hill was the dominant female golfer in the two Carolinas and one of the most outstanding players in the world. She was the winner of numerous amateur championships. Photograph courtesy North Carolina Collection.

Many colleges had golf programs by the 1930s, although the sport had neither the popularity nor the sophistication it would later achieve in the state. Most of the state's courses established a variety of local tournaments, which helped generate interest in the sport. Slowly but surely golf in North Carolina was becoming less of a country-club pastime and more of a competitive sport. The somewhat more open doors of the golfing world still did not admit blacks, however, who were generally absent from competitive circles.

Tennis, like golf, expanded somewhat from its patrician origins in the interwar period. Golf center Pinehurst was also an important locale for tennis with its annual North and South championships, which attracted such notables as Bill Tilden and Vincent Richards. The North Carolina Open Championships were held in Asheville during this period, while the Middle Atlantic Tournament in Charlotte started in 1925. In 1927 the North Carolina State Closed Championships were begun in Raleigh.

North Carolina's black tennis players were forced to play in the segregated American Tennis Association. A pair of talented brothers from Wilmington, Nathaniel and Franklin Jackson, dominated the association's national championships in the 1930s.

The University of North Carolina had the dominant college tennis program in this period. Under the tutelage of coach John Kenfield the Tar Heels were unbeaten in dual meets from 1930 through 1933, 1936, 1937, and 1939 through 1941. The most successful UNC player was Bitsy Grant, who after the close of his college career won three National Clay Court championships and was a member of four United States Davis Cup teams. Duke and Davidson were occasionally competitive with UNC.

Football, baseball, basketball, golf, and tennis were only a few of the sports played on the state's campuses. Most schools fielded teams in track and field, cross-country, swimming, wrestling, and boxing. Many of these so-called minor sports depended on scholarship football players for their best athletes and football revenues for their operating expenses. The precarious economy of the 1930s placed these nonrevenue sports on shaky footing. At North Carolina State, for example, the track and cross-country teams were essentially discontinued for most of the 1930s.

UNC's Bob Fetzer was the state's most successful track coach. His best-known athlete was UNC runner Harry Williamson, who finished sixth at 800 meters for the United States in the Berlin Olympics in 1936. Davidson hurdler Heath Whittle attracted national attention in the late 1930s, while North Carolina State football player Jack McDowall was almost as well known for his track exploits as his gridiron feats. These men were exceptions, however, as relatively few North Carolinians achieved national-class track performances during this period.

By the 1930s most of the state's coeducational colleges and universities had physical education and intramural programs for their women students, but, in general, opportunities for intercollegiate competition were limited to men. Even the state's female colleges provided only limited intercollegiate opportunities. At Raleigh's Meredith College, for example, the highlight of the athletic season in the 1920s was the intramural Field Day. By the 1930s Meredith students could participate in tennis, basketball, field hockey, soccer, volleyball, swimming, and golf, although mostly in an intramural context. East Carolina Teachers College, largely female at this time, started an intercollegiate athletic program in the middle 1930s that included teams in basketball, volleyball, and tennis. Difficulties in finding opponents and persistent doubts as to the appropriateness of women's athletics led to the suspension of the program by the end of the 1930s.

Horse racing continued to decline in popularity and importance in the state. Although racing continued at the State Fair and county fairs, North Carolina was largely bypassed by the national horse-racing community, which sought out areas more congenial to the formalized gambling connected with the sport. Another type of racing experienced a false start around this time. In 1924 the 1¼ - mile Charlotte Speedway was opened. The speedway, a board track built of green pine and cypress, hosted not stock car racing, which did not arrive until the late 1940s, but rather Indianapolis-style automobile racing. Unfortunately the wooden track began to deteriorate in the 1930s when Depression economics made its repair unfeasible. In the 1940s the track's lumber was donated to the war effort.

Hunting and fishing were activities likewise forced to make peace with the new age of bureaucracy. The urban redistribution of population, increased protectionist impulses, and the belated realization that the state's supply of game was not infinite mandated increased control. In 1927 the General Assembly established the State Game Commission. The new organization took over administration of hunting and fishing regulations in North Carolina from the Audubon Society. The commission expanded the licensing system to include North Carolina residents and began the task of replenishing dwindling game stocks.

The Second World War basically shut down sports in the United States. Major league baseball and professional football continued, but without most of their better players. In North Carolina college athletic programs, minor league baseball, golf tournaments, and other activities were either de-emphasized or discontinued. By 1943 many of the best athletes in the state were located not on college campuses but on military installations.

VI: 1945-1988

In 1946 the United States was free from depression and war for the first time in nearly two decades. The resulting pent-up desire for recreation and leisure helped propel spectator sports in North Carolina and throughout the United States to an enormous expansion, a growth that shows no sign of abatement more than four decades later. More fans follow more sports with greater intensity and enthusiasm than ever before. These sports are likewise covered by more media in greater detail than ever before. New technologies have helped make sports a pervasive part of American society and saturated the sporting world with massive amounts of money.

The 1950 census enumerated more than one million urban Tar Heels for the first time. With this increased urbanization came a continued growth of middle-class leisure time. Likewise, the phenomenal postwar expansion of the state's colleges and universities created new demands and new opportunities for recreation.

Much of this new leisure time was spent watching that marvel of mid-twentieth-century technology, television. The influence of television on modern sports can hardly be overstated. Since the nineteenth century, technologies such as the railroad, the telegraph, the automobile, and radio have conquered time and distance and brought the sporting world closer together. None of these had the profound effect of television, however. Tar Heel sports fans who had never seen a major league baseball game or a pro football contest in person could now watch the World Series, the Rose Bowl, the Masters, or even the Olympics in the comfort of their living room. By the 1980s and the advent of cablevision, superstations, and satellite dishes, virtually every sporting event of consequence was televised. Television helped the National Football League overtake major league baseball as the premier sports league in the United States. In North Carolina the Atlantic Coast Conference's decision to create a regional basketball network helped that young league establish local dominance. The enormous amount of money spent by television on sports has raised professional salaries, subsidized college athletic programs, and spurred a winning-at-all-costs mentality. Television money has also tended to make the rich richer and the poor poorer. National broadcasts of major league games helped send minor league baseball into a thirty-year downward spiral. The concentration on major college football and basketball programs has increased the gap between the larger schools and their smaller cousins and diminished the relative stature of other campus sports. Specialized newspapers and magazines have been instrumental in saturating the sporting public with information.

As technology has helped expand the sporting world, it has also helped bring it closer together. Virtually every local sporting activity in North Carolina is somehow tied in to a larger national or even international bureaucracy. Skilled college teams or individuals strive for an appearance in the national championships of the NCAA or NAIA. In many sports the elite can represent the United States in the Olympics or other international competition. Minor league baseball teams and players are under contract to major league franchises. Athletes strive to make their fortune in the baseball major leagues, the National Football League (NFL), the National Basketball Association (NBA), the Professional Golf Association (PGA), the World Circuit of Tennis (WCT), or any of a number of other professional sports associations and leagues. This growth of bureaucracy can be seen graphically in the development of college athletic departments, with athletic directors, assistant athletic directors, scores of head and assistant coaches, sports information departments, secretaries, ticket managers, and fund-raising booster clubs that may or may not be under the control of the athletic department. Most colleges combine with likeminded schools to form athletic conferences, which are part of either the NCAA or NAIA. These college bureaucracies have combined in recent years to produce a dizzying array of rules changes involving recruiting, eligibility, scheduling, television, scholarship limitations, and red-shirting (extending eligibility to a fifth year) in a not-always-successful attempt to control the athletic beast and equalize opportunities for competition.

Another profound change in American sports is racial integration. This phenomenon took place over a two-decade period and was not without the bitterness and struggle encountered in other aspects of the civil rights movement. In general pro sports integrated sooner than college sports, at least in the South. Major league baseball and professional football were integrated shortly after World War II, while the National Basketball Association followed suit in 1950. The professional golf tour, on the other hand, remained overwhelmingly white well into the 1960s. Baseball's southern minor leagues, such as those in North Carolina, did not become integrated until the 1950s or later, while most of the state's colleges did not have black football or basketball players until the latter part of that decade. Few blacks have been head coaches or athletic administrators at predominantly white schools.

In some sports women's entry into big-time sports was delayed longer than that of blacks. Women were long restricted to such sports as golf, tennis, and bowling, which were perceived to be less physically demanding and more ladylike than others. An example of this attitude can be seen in Olympic track and field competition, which as late as 1956 had no women's race longer than 200 meters—under the theory that longer races were too difficult and dangerous for frail females.

The American higher educational system had little to offer in the way of women's intercollegiate sports. This began to change in the 1970s under the influence of the women's movement. The most profound aspect of this change was the passage of the 1972 Educational Amendments Act. Title IX of this bill outlawed sexual discrimination by any educational institution that received federal funds. The Association for Intercollegiate Athletics for Women (AIAW) conducted national championships for colleges before being absorbed by the NCAA in the early 1980s. By the 1980s North Carolina colleges had dozens of scholarship women athletes competing for conference and regional championships, while the NCAA conducted national championships for women in basketball, golf, tennis, track and field, cross-country, swimming and diving, volleyball, and other sports. The International Olympic Committee has likewise responded to the changing climate and has expanded women's opportunities in the Olympics. Nonetheless, women's sports rank behind men's sports in media attention, crowd size, and financial rewards. Particularly obvious is the lack of professional team-sports opportunities for post-college women athletes. Equally obvious is the continuing progress made by women's athletics in the period since Title IX revolutionized college sports in the United States.

Black or white, male or female, athletes in the post-World War II era have progressively started earlier, specialized more, and trained more scientifically. Exposure to coaching at an earlier age, as well as technological and training innovations, including sophisticated weight lifting, have led to better performances and increased skills. This greater professionalization has in turn led to increased distance between the upper echelon of skilled participants and lesser skilled spectators and has widened further the gap between spectator and participant sports.

Immediately following World War II, baseball remained the preferred sport in the United States and North Carolina. Indeed, the end of a long period of depression and war, the return of major league stars from the war, and the gradual arrival of the cream of the Negro Leagues helped make the late 1940s something of a golden age for baseball. This enthusiastic interest in baseball was duplicated in the minors. By 1949 some fifty-nine minor leagues were in operation throughout the nation. In North Carolina forty-nine minor league teams operated in the following leagues: Carolina, North Carolina State, Coastal Plains, Tobacco State, Blue Ridge, Tar Heel, Tri-State, and Western Carolina. Professional baseball could be found not only in the state's large cities—Charlotte, Raleigh, Durham, Greensboro, and Winston-Salem—but also in such seemingly unlikely locales as Ayden, Edenton, Landis, Lincolnton, Marion, and Snow Hill.

One result of this phenomenal expansion was a dilution of talent and a devaluation of statistics. During these years some rather unexceptional ballplayers compiled some exceptional seasons. In 1946, for example, pitcher William Kennedy of the Coastal Plains League Rocky Mount team won 28 and lost 3, with an earned run average of 1.03 and an extraordinary 456 strikeouts. Two years later Rocky Mount's Horace Benton won 28 and lost but 10, while in 1950 Roanoke Rapids's Alton Brown, also of the Coastal Plains League, went 28-11. On the other side of the plate .400 hitters were almost common, led by Hickory's "Pud" Miller, who batted .425 with 40 home runs and 136 runs batted in in the 1951 North Carolina State League. In 1948 Floyd Yount of Newton-Conover, in the Western Carolina League, batted .420 and hit 43 home runs. That same year forty-year-old player-manager Wes Ferrell, the former big league pitching star, batted .425 in the WCL. In 1949 Leo (Muscle) Shoals powered 55 home runs for Reidsville in the Carolina League. With the exception of Ferrell, none of these players ever made the major leagues. Some future big league standouts did play in the state during this period, however. They included Al Rosen and Eddie Mathews (Thomasville), Harvey Haddix (Winston-Salem), Gus Zernial (Burlington), Hoyt Wilhelm (Mooresville), and Ray Jablonski (Winston-Salem).

The phenomenal resurgence of minor league ball was short-lived, however. The major culprits were television, which broadcast major league games into every area of the state, and the continuing growth in popularity of other sports such as football, basketball, and golf. Most of the state's minor leagues and teams disappeared in the 1950s.

The major survivor was the Carolina League, whose teams represented most of the state's largest cities, including Durham, Greensboro, Winston-Salem, and Fayetteville. The Carolina League was founded in 1945 as an eight-team league of North Carolina and Virginia cities. It varied from six to ten teams from its founding through the 1974 season. By 1975 it was barely holding on, with only four teams. In 1976 and 1977 Winston- Salem was the only North Carolina city left in an otherwise all-Virginia league. This was the bottom of the trough, however. Since 1977 the Carolina League has ranged from six to eight teams in North Carolina, Virginia, and occasionally Maryland. The Durham Bulls returned in 1980 and have been a model team during the 1980s, leading all Class A (the smallest minor league classification except rookie leagues) teams in attendance several times, while Winston-Salem has remained a league bulwark. In 1988 the Bulls, bolstered by the popularity of the movie *Bull Durham*, set a Class A season attendance record of more than 270,000 paying customers.

Other leagues are represented by North Carolina cities. Charlotte has been a member of either the South Atlantic League or the Southern

League under the ownership of the Crockett family. Presently Charlotte plays in the Double A Southern League. Asheville likewise spent time in several associations before settling in the South Atlantic League. This league has undergone expansion in recent years and now challenges the Carolina League throughout much of the state. Greensboro, Fayetteville, and Gastonia have joined Asheville in that circuit, which also includes teams from South Carolina, West Virginia, and Georgia. Although there is no reason to suspect a return to the halcyon days of the late 1940s, minor league baseball does appear to have regained a secure niche in the middle of the state's sporting hierarchy.

Despite the up-and-down roller coaster ride of minor league baseball, it has continued to be the most successful incubator of major league talent, a fact that has guaranteed major league subsidy and survival. Although a few independents surface now and then, most teams in recent years have been "farm" teams of big league franchises: a system whereby the major league team subsidizes the minor league team in exchange for control of player contracts. North Carolina minor leagues have not been in the highest classification (those closest to the majors), and most players, even stars, have spent their careers in the minors. The state's minor league parks, have, however, nurtured their share of future big league stars. During the 1950s and 1960s the Carolina League featured a number of future big league standouts. Curt Flood (High Point-Thomasville) led the league with a .340 average in 1956, while in 1959 Carl Yastrzemski started his illustrious pro career with a .377 average for Raleigh. Gates Brown of Durham and Cesar Tovar of Rocky Mount led the league in batting in 1961 and 1962 on the way to solid big league careers. Other future big leaguers of the 1960s with North Carolina experience included Al Oliver, Richie Hebner, Gene Garber, Manny Sanguillen, and Dick

One of the greatest competitors to play minor league baseball in North Carolina was Carl Yastrzemski, standout player for the Boston Red Sox during the 1960s and 1970s. Yastrzemski had a superb season with the Raleigh Capitals in 1959. Photograph (April, 1959) from the Raleigh *News and Observer* Negative File in the custody of the Archives, Division of Archives and History.

Radatz of Raleigh; Bobby Murcer, Roy White, Tom Tresh, Mel Stottlemyre, and Jim Bouton of Greensboro; Joe Morgan, Rusty Staub, and Mickey Lolich of Durham; Rod Carew of Wilson; Rico Petrocelli, Sparky Lyle, Wilbur Wood, and George Scott of Winston-Salem; Lee May and Tony Perez of Rocky Mount; Steve Blass of Kinston; and Greg Luzinski of Raleigh-Durham.

Much of the nucleus of the outstanding Minnesota Twins teams of the 1960s prepped at Charlotte and included Bob Allison; Harmon Killebrew, who hit 15 home runs in a half-season in 1956; and Tony Oliva, who batted .350 in 1962. Graig Nettles later played in Charlotte, while Willie Stargell played for Asheville. Western Carolina League players include Bobby Bonds of Lexington, Gene Tenace of Shelby, and Richie Zisk of Gastonia. This trend has continued into the 1970s and 1980s. Among the top current major league players to have played minor league ball in North Carolina are Don Mattingly and Mike Pagliarulo (Greensboro); Wade Boggs and John Tudor (Winston-Salem); Eddie Murray and Cal Ripken (Charlotte); Dave Righetti (Asheville); Jesse Barfield (Kinston); Brett Butler, Gerald Perry, and Brian Fisher (Durham); and Andy Van Slyke (Gastonia).

After the war North Carolina continued to send players to the major leagues in large numbers. Enos (Country) Slaughter of Roxboro was a colorful outfielder whose multiple skills led to a Hall of Fame career. He had a lifetime average of .300 with 2,383 hits in a nineteen-year career. Other prominent Tar Heels in the 1950s include Smokey Burgess, a catcher from Caroleen, who batted .295 for his career; Billy Goodman of Concord, who led the American League with a .354 average in 1950 and compiled a .300 lifetime average; Whitey Lockman of Lowell, a member of the 1954 World Series champion New York Giants, who hit a lifetime .279 with 1,658 hits and 114 home runs; and Johnny Temple of Lexington, a career .284 hitter with 1,484 hits.

In the 1960s and 1970s, most of the better North Carolinians in the majors were pitchers. Perhaps the most popular was Hertford's Jim (Catfish) Hunter, who gained a reputation as a premier "money" pitcher. Hunter won 224 regular-season games and five World Series games for the Oakland Athletics and New York Yankees in a distinguished career that led to his induction into baseball's Hall of Fame. He pitched a rare perfect game for Oakland in 1968 and in 1974 was named recipient of the American League Cy Young Award, presented annually to the best pitcher in each league. Hunter also became baseball's first high-priced free agent. In a landmark court decision in 1974 he won his freedom from Oakland and signed a precedent-setting $3.75 million free-agent contract with the Yankees.

Joining Hunter in the Hall of Fame is Huntersville's Hoyt Wilhelm, the first relief pitcher so honored. A knuckleball specialist, Wilhelm pitched in 1,070 games, a major league record (since broken), in an outstanding

Enos (Country) Slaughter of Roxboro was a noted outfielder in the 1940s and 1950s who achieved a lifetime batting average of .300 and membership in the National Baseball Hall of Fame. Photograph courtesy National Baseball Library.

Cy Young Award winner and Hall of Famer Jim (Catfish) Hunter, originally from Hertford, had a distinguished pitching career in major league baseball in the 1960s and 1970s. Photograph courtesy National Baseball Library.

Famed relief pitcher and knuckleballer Hoyt Wilhelm of Huntersville is also a member of the National Baseball Hall of Fame. He pitched in more than 1,000 games during an outstanding twenty-year career. Photograph courtesy National Baseball Library.

Strikeout ace Gaylord Perry of Williamston, winner of 300 games and two Cy Young awards, will almost certainly be inducted into the National Baseball Hall of Fame. His older brother, Jim, was likewise a recipient of the Cy Young award. Photograph supplied by the North Carolina Sports Hall of Fame.

big-league career that lasted from 1952 until 1972 and included 143 wins and 227 saves. Williamston brothers Gaylord and Jim Perry became the only siblings to win the Cy Young Award. Older brother Jim won 267, lost 206, and won the Cy Young in 1970 for the Minnesota Twins. Gaylord Perry had 314 career wins and a staggering 3,534 strikeouts. He captured Cy Young awards in 1972 for Cleveland and in 1978 for San Diego. He was also one of the most colorful and controversial players of his time because of his alleged skill in throwing the spitball and other illegal pitches. Despite the controversy, Perry's status as a 300-game winner likely ensures his future induction into the Hall of Fame. Other standout North Carolina-born pitchers during this period include Tarboro's Mike Caldwell, Lincolnton's Tony Cloninger, Jim Bibby of Franklinton, and relief ace Ted Abernathy of Stanley.

No North Carolina hitters during this period approached the stature of pitchers Hunter, Wilhelm, or the Perry brothers. Tar Heels who had solid careers included George Altman of Goldsboro, Wes Covington of Laurinburg, Jimmie Hall of Mount Holly, Jim Ray Hart of Hookerton, Tommy Helms of Charlotte, and Chuck Hinton of Rocky Mount.

In recent years, as basketball, golf, and other sports have gained in popularity, the number of North Carolinians in the major leagues has declined dramatically. By the late 1980s only a handful of Tar Heels, including Scott Bankhead of Raleigh, Franklin Stubbs of Laurinburg, Mark Grace of Winston-Salem, Otis Nixon of Columbus County, and Mike LaValliere of Charlotte, were in the big leagues. Perhaps the most successful North Carolinians in the majors in the 1980s are managers Hal Lanier (Denton), who led the Houston Astros to the 1986 National League West title, and Roger Craig (Durham), who duplicated that feat with the 1987 San Francisco Giants.

With the relative decline of minor league baseball in the 1950s, the opportunity was open for the area's colleges to fortify their dominant position in spectator sports in the state. The postwar influx of veterans into the state's colleges and universities touched off an enrollment boom that continued for decades after the close of the war. This dramatic increase in the number of students was followed in due course by an equally dramatic increase in the number of alumni. The continued increase in the quality of the state's road system, the establishment of statewide college-sport radio networks, increased television coverage, sophisticated sports information departments, and newer and larger facilities, particularly for basketball, all enabled larger and larger numbers of fans to follow their favorite teams more easily. Shorter work weeks made it more feasible for fans to attend contests conveniently scheduled for weekends or nights. It became increasingly common for fans and alumni from across the state to converge on the state's college campuses for the big game.

The big game, however, was a football game or, later, a basketball game. College baseball remained a minor sport on the state's campuses, generally being played before modest crowds and receiving little media attention. Nonetheless, the state produced some standout teams. Wake Forest won the NCAA tournament in 1955, the only North Carolina or ACC team to accomplish that feat. Duke, coached by Ace Parker, one of its greatest athletes, was a national power in the 1950s. In 1967 former big leaguer Sam Esposito became head coach at North Carolina State. His 1968 Wolfpack nine advanced to the College World Series, where they finished third. Esposito's teams continued to be frequent visitors to the NCAA tournament throughout the 1970s and 1980s. UNC advanced to the College World Series in 1960, 1966, and 1978, while East Carolina won the NAIA national championship in 1961. Among the many North Carolina collegians to advance to the majors were 1960 National League Most Valuable Player Dick Groat of Duke; Mike Caldwell, Tim Stoddard, and Dan Plesac of North Carolina State; Gaylord Perry of Campbell; B. J. Surhoff, Scott Bankhead, Walt Weiss, and Scott Bradley of UNC; and Al Holland of North Carolina A&T. Surhoff and Bankhead made the 1984 United States Olympic baseball team, while Wake Forest's Bill Masse made the 1988 team. Weiss, a shortstop for the Oakland Athletics, won the American League Rookie of the Year award for 1988.

Like minor league baseball, college football underwent a boom period after the war. Unlike minor league baseball, however, college football has retained its popularity. Football at UNC reached its high-water mark in the late 1940s. In 1945 Carl Snavely returned to Chapel Hill from Cornell. The following year, relying heavily on returning GI's, Snavely began fashioning a powerhouse that included UNC's first three bowl teams. Snavely was a master of the single-wing offense, which rarely worked better than it did at Chapel Hill in the 1946-1949 period. The most important cog in Snavely's single-wing machine was Asheville's all-American Charlie Justice, a remarkably gifted and versatile runner, passer, punter, and kick returner. The legendary Justice combined his skills with the rabid enthusiasm for college football of the period to become arguably the most famous athlete in the state's history. Indeed, Justice's stature tended to obscure the considerable skills of such fellow Tar Heels as all-American ends Art Weiner and Ken Powell.

In 1946 UNC compiled an impressive record of 8-1-1 before losing 20-10 to Georgia in the Sugar Bowl, Carolina's first post-season bowl game. The team followed with an 8-2 season in 1947, which was not rewarded with a bowl trip. In 1948 Carolina went 9-0-1 before a 14-6 loss to Oklahoma in the Sugar Bowl. Justice's last season, 1949, ended with a somewhat disappointing regular-season record of 7-3 and a 23-13 loss to Rice in the Cotton Bowl. Justice finished second in the balloting for the Heisman Trophy in 1948 and 1949; this attainment remains the highest finish by a North Carolinian in the voting for that prestigious award, given to the nation's outstanding college player.

The UNC football career of Charlie (Choo Choo) Justice of Asheville remains legendary on the Chapel Hill campus. Justice, an all-American, finished second in the balloting for the prestigious Heisman Trophy in 1948 and 1949. Photograph from the files of the Division of Archives and History.

Snavely was unable to maintain the program at this level, however. A series of disputes, including the size of the recruiting budget and Snavely's reluctance to abandon the single wing, helped lead to losing records in the early 1950s. Snavely left Carolina under fire after the 1952 season. Following Snavely's departure, UNC wandered in the football wilderness for the next decade and a half. UNC alumni George Barclay and Jim Tatum failed to return the Tar Heels to glory, although Tatum, who had coached Maryland with great distinction, appeared to be heading in a positive direction until his untimely death in 1959. His replacement, Jim Hickey, had an eight-year career losing record. The one break in this string of mediocrity was the 1963 season. Led by the fine play of future NFL stars Ken Willard and Chris Hanburger, UNC went 8-2 and finished the season with an impressive 35-0 thumping of the Air Force Academy in the Gator Bowl.

In 1967 Bill Dooley became head coach at UNC. After several struggling seasons Dooley returned the program to national prominence. The Tar Heels went to six bowl games in the 1970s under Dooley, although they won only once. This succession of bowl teams was highlighted by a 1972 team that went 10-1 in regular season and won the Sun Bowl 32-28 over Texas Tech. Dooley's teams featured a succession of outstanding running backs such as Don McCauley, who rushed for 1,720 yards and scored 21 touchdowns in 1970, and Mike Voight, who finished his UNC career in 1976 with 3,971 career rushing yards.

Dooley left UNC after 1977 to become the head football coach and athletic director at Virginia Tech. He was replaced by Dick Crum, who was hired from Miami of Ohio. During Crum's generally successful tenure UNC locked horns with the nation's elite in post-season bowl appearances in 1979, 1980, 1981, 1982, 1983, and 1986. The 1980 Tar Heel team, led by offensive linemen Ron Wooten and Rick Donnelly, standout linebacker Lawrence Taylor, and running backs Amos Lawrence and Kelvin Bryant, fashioned a 10-1 regular season record, losing only to Oklahoma, and finished with a 16-7 Bluebonnet Bowl triumph over Texas. Crum's conservative offense subsequently lost favor with some UNC fans, and he was dismissed at the conclusion of a losing 1987 season. Under new coach Mack Brown, the Tar Heels staggered through a dismal 1-10 season in 1988.

Although Duke did not regain its prewar level of success, it did remain a national football power into the 1960s. Wallace Wade returned from the war in 1946 and remained through 1950, winning only a disappointing 25 games in 5 years. He left coaching to become commissioner of the Southern Conference and was replaced by former Duke player Bill Murray. Murray coached at Duke through the 1965 season, leaving with a record of 93-51-9. His Duke teams won the Southern Conference championship in 1952 and won or shared the ACC title, 1953-1955 and 1960-1962. During his tenure Duke played in three bowls, winning twice. Murray had a number of all-Americans, most notably Ed Meadows, Mike McGee, Tee Moorman, Jean Berry, and Jay Wilkinson. Defensive lineman McGee won the Outland Trophy, awarded to the nation's best lineman, in 1959.

After the 1965 season Murray resigned to become executive director of the American Football Coaches Association. After his departure the Duke administration flirted periodically with de-emphasizing college football, a move never completed. One manifestation of this sentiment, however, was the hiring of Tom Harp to replace Murray. Harp had an undistinguished record at Cornell and was hired largely on the basis of his Ivy League credentials. His contract was not renewed after four seasons produced a 22-28-1 record. His replacement was former Duke star McGee, a defense-oriented coach who was unable to do better than 6-5 records compiled in 1971 and 1974. McGee left under fire after a 4-7 season in 1978 reduced his overall Duke record to 37-47-4. Neither "Red" Wilson, 1979-1982, nor Steve Sloan, 1983-1986, was able to return Duke to its previous glory. Former Heisman Trophy winner Steve Spurrier became head coach in 1987. In his second season he coached the Blue Devils to a 7-3-1 record, their best showing since 1962.

During the post-Murray years Duke's program has produced a number of exceptional players, although not enough to produce winning seasons routinely. Defensive back Ernie Jackson was ACC Player of the

Year in 1971, an award also won by running back Steve Jones in 1972, wide receiver Chris Castor in 1982, quarterback Ben Bennett in 1983, and quarterback Anthony Dilweg in 1988. Bennett passed for 9,614 career yards, an NCAA record in 1983, since broken, while Dilweg threw for an ACC single-season record 3,824 yards in 1988. Duke won the College Football Association's award for football academic excellence three times in the 1980s.

North Carolina State struggled against UNC and Duke for many years. Tiny Riddick Field made it difficult to fill the athletic coffers and attract quality athletes, while a limited curriculum heavy on engineering further hindered recruiting. Several coaches labored against these handicaps and occasionally produced some fine teams. In 1946 State, coached by former Chicago Bears standout Beattie Feathers, went 8-2 and played in its first bowl game, a 34-13 Gator Bowl loss to Oklahoma. This success was short-lived, however. The program bottomed out in the early 1950s as State went 9-31 from 1951 through 1954 under three coaches. Earle Edwards, coach from 1954 until 1970, succeeded in stabilizing the program. The 1957 Wolfpack, which went 7-1-2 and won the ACC championship, was led by halfback Dick Christy, who was named all-American and ACC Player of the Year. In 1960 State was 6-3-1 and boasted one of the nation's outstanding quarterbacks, rifle-armed Roman Gabriel, who was named ACC Player of the Year, an honor he claimed again the following year. In 1963 State was 8-2 and ACC co-champion; it lost 16-12 to Mississippi State in the Liberty Bowl that year. The 1967 team, led by defensive tackle Dennis Byrd, won its first eight games and climbed to the high regions of the wire-service polls before close losses to Penn State and Clemson finished the regular season. The season ended on a high note, however, with a 14-7 victory over Georgia in the Liberty Bowl, State's first bowl victory.

Riddick Field was finally retired after the 1965 season, when Carter Stadium (now Carter-Finley Stadium) was completed. The new stadium and a broader curriculum enabled NCSU to compete more successfully in the recruiting arena. The benefits were first reaped by Lou Holtz, a dynamic, offensive-minded coach who came to State in 1972. His first Wolfpack team went 7-3-1 and defeated West Virginia 49-13 in the Peach Bowl. Holtz's Wolfpack followed up 1972 with successive seasons of 8-3, 8-2-1, and 7-3-1, all resulting in bowl appearances.

Holtz left State after the 1975 season and was replaced by assistant Bo Rein. Under the leadership of Rein and the talent of running back Ted Brown and offensive lineman Jim Richter, winner of the 1979 Outland Trophy, State returned to postseason bowls in 1977 and 1978. Rein left State for the head coaching job at Louisiana State University after a 7-4 ACC championship season in 1979 and subsequently was killed in an airplane crash. Neither his replacement, Monte Kiffin (1980-1982), nor Kiffin's replacement, Tom Reed (1983-1985), could return the State program to the level of success it enjoyed in the 1970s. In 1986 Dick Sheridan became head coach at State. In his first season he coached the Wolfpack to a surprising 8-2-1 regular season record and a last-second Peach Bowl loss to Virginia Tech. Wolfpack quarterback Eric Kramer was ACC Player of the Year. After the 1988 season, State returned to the Peach Bowl, where it defeated Iowa.

Wake Forest was coached by Douglas Clyde (Peahead) Walker after the war. Walker took the Deacons to the first Gator Bowl game, a 26-14 Deacon victory over South Carolina, following the 1945 season. Three years later Wake Forest lost 20-7 to Baylor in the Dixie Bowl. Walker left over a salary squabble after the 1950 season. The small Baptist school had many lean years following Walker's departure. Wake Forest seriously considered de-emphasizing football in the early 1970s. Even during its slack years, however, Wake Forest had some stars, including quarterback Norm Snead, running backs Billy Barnes and Brian Piccolo, and defensive back Bill Armstrong. Generally a passing team during this period, Wake Forest relied heavily on such quarterbacks as Snead, Jay Venuto, and Mike Elkins. Among Wake's standout years was a surprise ACC championship team in 1970, ironically a running team led by tailback Larry Hopkins. In 1979 the Deacons made it to its second bowl game, a one-sided Tangerine Bowl loss to Louisiana State University. The loss, however, took little of the luster off a standout 8-3 regular season, coached by former Wake Forest quarterback John Mackovic and led by Venuto and running back James McDougald. In 1987 former UNC and Virginia Tech coach Bill Dooley took over at Wake Forest and produced records of 7-4 and 6-4-1 in his first two outings.

In the 1940s and 1950s North Carolina college football was focused on the so-called Big Four of UNC, Duke, North Carolina State, and Wake Forest. In the 1960s that changed as East Carolina made a bold move for the big time. School president Leo Jenkins felt that a big-time program would give the school greater visibility and credibility while increasing financial support. Jenkins hired coach Clarence Stasavich from Lenoir Rhyne in 1962, one year before Ficklen Stadium opened on the ECU campus. In 1963 East Carolina went 9-1, including a 20-10 victory over Wake Forest, and played in the Eastern Bowl, defeating Northeastern 27-6. In 1964 the Pirates again went 9-1 and defeated Massachusetts 14-13 in the Tangerine Bowl. A third straight 9-1 season in 1965 led to a 31-0 victory over Maine in the Tangerine Bowl.

East Carolina joined the Southern Conference in 1964, enlarged Ficklen Stadium, and began playing bigger-name schools. Sonny Randle coached back-to-back 9-2 seasons in 1972 and 1973, while Pat Dye coached from 1974 to 1979 with a record of 48-18-1, including a victory over Louisiana Tech in the 1978 Independence Bowl. Quarterback Carl Summerell, running back Carlester Crumpler, and linebacker Danny Kepley were Pirate standouts in the early 1970s. East Carolina proved

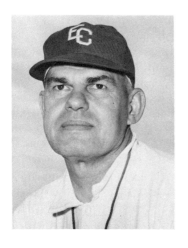

Clarence Stasavich became head football coach at East Carolina University in Greenville in 1962 and led the Pirates on a three-year-long winning spree. Photograph courtesy Pirate Sports Information, East Carolina University.

increasingly competitive against their Big Four opponents, all of whom, with the exception of North Carolina State, quickly dropped the Pirates from their schedules. East Carolina withdrew from the Southern Conference following the 1976 season and has played as an independent since.

Dye's replacement, Ed Emory, coached the Pirates to winning seasons in 1982 and 1983. But Emory lost popularity quickly after losing seasons in 1984 and 1985 and was replaced by Art Baker, who had problems with the lack of conference affiliation and a difficult schedule and left after the 1988 season. The increasingly bitter State-ECU rivalry was terminated, at least temporarily, after the 1987 game ended with clashes involving fans and security personnel.

The state's smaller schools have occasionally attracted the attention usually reserved for the larger schools. Lenoir Rhyne was NAIA runner-up in 1959, champion in 1960, and runner-up in 1962. The Bears were coached by Clarence Stasavich, later of East Carolina. Elon finished runner-up in the NAIA championship under Red Wilson in 1973 and 1978 before winning the championship under Jerry Tolley in 1980 and 1981. Western Carolina finished runner-up in the NCAA-1AA finals in 1983, while Appalachian State advanced to the NCAA-1AA semifinals in 1987. North Carolina A&T and North Carolina Central have continued a fierce rivalry.

Numerous North Carolina collegians have found fame and fortune in the professional ranks. Wake Forest's Bill George was a standout linebacker for the Chicago Bears from 1952 until 1965 and is a member of the Pro Football Hall of Fame. North Carolina State's Alex Webster was an outstanding fullback for the championship New York Giants in the late 1950s and 1960s, while former Duke linemen Al DeRogatis and Ed Meadows were all-star linemen in the 1950s. UNC's Charlie Justice was unable to duplicate his college success in the NFL.

Three of the most successful quarterbacks of the 1960s were Big Four alumni. The most unlikely of these was Sonny Jurgenson, who had an unexceptional football career at Duke. Nonetheless, the strong-armed Wilmington native was a superb quarterback with the Philadelphia Eagles and Washington Redskins and is a member of the Pro Football Hall of

In spite of an unexceptional football career at Duke University, Wilmington native Sonny Jurgenson (facing camera) went on to distinguish himself as a quarterback for the Philadelphia Eagles and the Washington Redskins during the 1960s and 1970s. Jurgenson is a member of the Pro Football Hall of Fame. Photograph supplied by the North Carolina Sports Hall of Fame.

Fame. He concluded his career with more than 32,000 passing yards and 255 touchdown passes and ranks in the top ten in every major NFL career passing statistic. North Carolina State's Roman Gabriel, also a native of Wilmington, quarterbacked for the Los Angeles Rams and Philadelphia Eagles from 1962 until 1977, accumulating more than 29,000 passing yards and completing 201 touchdown passes. In 1969 Gabriel led the Rams to an 11-2-1 record and was named the league's Most Valuable Player, the first ACC player to be so honored. Wake Forest's Norm Snead passed for 196 touchdowns and more than 30,000 yards in his NFL career.

Other top-level NFL players of this period with North Carolina college connections include defensive linemen John Baker of Raleigh and North Carolina Central and Jethro Pugh of Elizabeth City State, standout linebackers Mike Curtis and Bob Matheson of Duke and Chris Hanburger of UNC, running backs Ken Willard (6,105 career rushing yards, 277 career pass receptions) and J. D. Smith (4,672 rushing yards) of North Carolina A&T, and offensive lineman Doug Wilkerson of North Carolina Central.

The outstanding former North Carolina college player in the NFL in the 1980s is former UNC linebacker Lawrence Taylor, a dominant defensive player for the New York Giants. In 1981 Taylor was named NFL

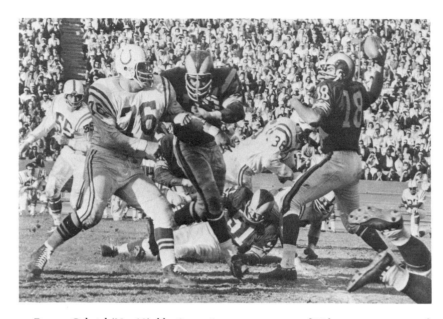

Roman Gabriel (No. 18), like Sonny Jurgenson a native of Wilmington, was a standout quarterback for North Carolina State University, the Los Angeles Rams, and the Philadelphia Eagles. In 1969 the National Football League named him its Most Valuable Player. Photograph from the files of the Division of Archives and History.

Rookie of the Year and Defensive Player of the Year. In 1986 he led the Giants to a Super Bowl victory and became one of the few defensive players to be named league MVP. Other former area collegians achieved all-star status in the 1980s. Former Duke players Ed Newman (Miami) and Billy Bryan (Denver) were among the NFL's top offensive linemen, as was former North Carolina State player Jim Richter for Buffalo. Former Wolfpacker Ted Brown rushed for more than 4,000 yards and caught 339 passes for Minnesota, while Philadelphia's Mike Quick, also from North Carolina State, emerged as a standout wide receiver in the middle 1980s.

College basketball in North Carolina got off to an auspicious beginning in the postwar era. In 1946 the UNC team, coached by Ben Carnevale and led by John (Hook) Dillon and Horace (Bones) McKinney, made it all the way to the championship game of the NCAA tournament, where they lost 43-40 to Oklahoma A&M (now Oklahoma State), coached by Henry Iba, the best-known coach of that era. UNC's postwar dominance in the state was short-lived, however. Coach Carnevale left for Navy after spending only two years in Chapel Hill. Contemporary with this departure was the arrival at North Carolina State of highly successful Indiana high school coach Everett Case. For a decade Case and his Wolfpack dominated basketball in the state and challenged Adolph Rupp's

This photograph of Everett Case was made on the day in 1946 that he joined North Carolina State College as head basketball coach. Shown in the background are the bare girders of Reynolds Coliseum, construction of which had begun in 1942 but was interrupted the following year by World War II. The coliseum opened in December, 1949, and became the scene of many basketball triumphs by Case-coached State teams. Photograph courtesy North Carolina State University; supplied by the North Carolina Sports Hall of Fame.

Kentucky dynasty for southern supremacy. Case introduced a fast-paced brand of basketball, featuring full-court presses and frequent fast breaks, recruited in an expanded and sophisticated national network, and toughened schedules. His outmatched rivals ultimately were forced to upgrade their programs in order to compete. For example, Case's State squad defeated arch rival UNC the first fifteen times they met.

Case's heyday was the decade from 1947 until 1956, during which he won 267 games against only 60 losses. From 1947 through 1953 State finished first in the Southern Conference regular season every year except 1952, when it was second to West Virginia. State won every post-season tournament from 1947 through 1952 before losing to Wake Forest 71-70 in the 1953 tournament final. Case's team then won the first three ACC tournaments in 1954, 1955, and 1956.

This gave Case nine conference championships in his first ten years, the sole loss being by one point. His star players during this period included Dick Dickey, Sammy Ranzino, Bobby Speight, Ronnie Shavlik, and Vic Molodet, all of whom received all-American honors. Reynolds Coliseum, which opened in 1949, hosted not only the Southern Conference tournament and then the Atlantic Coast Conference tournament but also the highly successful Dixie Classic, an eight-team holiday tournament in which the Big Four hosted four outside powers in a three-day extravaganza. Although North Carolina State was a perennial top-ten team, Case was unable to win the coveted national championship. The Wolfpack appeared in the NCAA tournament in 1950, 1951, 1952, 1954, and 1956 during a period in which that annual event involved considerably fewer teams than at present. State's best finish was in third place in 1950.

State's dominance during this period overshadowed some good basketball played elsewhere. Duke provided a stern rival in the early 1950s. Dick Groat, later a major league baseball star, was the nation's leading scorer in 1951 and an all-American guard in 1951 and 1952. Despite Groat's individual brilliance and a succession of twenty-win seasons, the Blue Devils were unable to advance to the NCAA, losing to State in the Southern Conference tournament finals in 1950, 1951, and 1952. In 1955, with State on probation, Duke made its first NCAA tournament appearance as conference runner-up, losing its opener to Villanova 74-73.

Wake Forest was also competitive during the early 1950s. The Deacons, who still shared Wake County with State, finally ended Case's dominance in the 1953 Southern Conference finals with a 71-70 victory. The following year State defeated Wake 82-80 in overtime in the first ACC tournament final. The most demonic Demon Deacon in the middle 1950s was Jonesville's Dickie Hemric, a burly all-American center who scored a still-unbroken ACC record 2,587 points in a four-year career ending in 1955.

State's archrival UNC chafed under the Wolfpack's dominance. In 1953 Carolina hired successful St. John's coach Frank McGuire to turn its fortunes around. McGuire quickly established a pipeline to the top prep talent in New York, the so-called "underground railroad." By 1956, the first year McGuire coached only his own recruits, UNC was 18-5. The following year the New York-dominated Tar Heel team came together in spectacular fashion. Led by all-American Lennie Rosenbluth (the Helms Foundation National Player of the Year), forward Pete Brennan, and playmaking guard Tommie Kearns, UNC swept through the regular season undefeated. In the tournament Carolina nipped Wake Forest 61-59 in a heart-stopping semifinal and then defeated South Carolina to qualify for the NCAA tournament. Victories over Yale, Canisius, and Syracuse gave the Tar Heels the Eastern Regional championship and sent them to Kansas City for the Final Four. North Carolina then won the national championship in a most improbable manner, victories in back-to-back triple overtime games. The first, a 74-70 win over Big Ten champion Michigan State, sent the Tar Heels into the finals against heavily favored Kansas, led by the already famous 7-foot Goliath Wilt Chamberlain. Carolina bottled up Chamberlain, survived the loss of Rosenbluth to fouls, and defeated the Jayhawks 54-53 on two last-second foul shots by Bob Quigg.

A valuable spin-off of the championship season was television. North Carolina's drive to the title was telecast throughout the state on an impromptu network set up by Castleman D. Chesley, a Philadelphia television executive. The following year Chesley and the league established a modest ACC network. Throughout the years this network developed into a lucrative venture and an influential factor in the growth of the ACC's popularity in the region.

By the late 1950s Case and McGuire faced increasingly difficult competition. In 1958 Duke finished in first place in the ACC regular season, while upstart Maryland won the tournament, the first non-Big Four team to do so. In 1959 Duke hired a young Case assistant, Vic Bubas, who won the tournament in 1960, his first try.

Duke University hired Vic Bubas, one of Everett Case's assistant coaches, as its head basketball coach in 1959. Bubas led the Blue Devils to an ACC tournament victory in his first year of coaching, and under his tutelage Duke dominated the ACC in the mid-1960s. Photograph courtesy Duke Sports Information.

By this time the ACC epitomized big-time college basketball: all-Americans; top-ten teams; large, enthusiastic crowds; and a television contract the envy of many an older league. An example of this ever-increasing popularity can be seen in Greensboro and Charlotte, two North Carolina cities not directly a part of the ACC, which by the early 1960s had begun a series of coliseum expansions in a largely successful attempt to attract ACC basketball. There was a dark side to this expansion, however. Allegations of improper recruiting plagued Case's high-powered program at State almost from the beginning. State was placed on probation for the 1955 season for recruiting irregularities and was unable to play in the NCAA play-offs despite a 28-4 record and an ACC tournament championship. This was just a prelude to a more serious affair involving Louisiana schoolboy standout Jackie Moreland in 1956. Following a variety of recruiting violations involving Moreland, State was placed on NCAA probation for four years, one of the stiffest penalties in NCAA history. In 1961 UNC was placed on one-year probation for excessive expenses involving recruiting. During the late 1950s and early 1960s the ACC was also plagued by a series of in-game fights involving practically every league team, especially McGuire's Tar Heels.

More serious than even the Moreland controversy was the point-shaving scandal of the early 1960s. Point shaving involved players accepting money from gamblers in return for assuring that their team's margin of victory or defeat was within a certain range. Four North Carolina State players accepted money to shave points in games from 1959 until 1961. A UNC player admitted to accepting bribes to fix games not involving his team, while other Tar Heel players failed to report attempted bribes. North Carolina Governor Terry Sanford and officials at both UNC and North Carolina State lost little time in reacting to the problem. They canceled the Dixie Classic and placed limitations in scheduling and recruiting on both schools. Although the recruiting and scheduling limitations were gradually lifted, the Dixie Classic was not revived.

The troubles at UNC and North Carolina State continued through the early 1960s. McGuire left for the NBA after the 1961 season, while Case was unable to recover from probation, scandal, and recruiting restrictions. This opened the door first for resurgent Wake Forest and then for Duke. Wake Forest, coached by colorful Bones McKinney and led by all-American center Len Chappell and guard Billy Packer, won the ACC tournament and advanced to the NCAA tournament in 1961 and 1962,

Wake Forest center and all-American Len Chappell (No. 51) led the Demon Deacons to ACC tournament victories and berths in the NCAA tournament in 1961 and 1962. During the latter season he averaged more than 30 points per game. Photograph supplied by the North Carolina Sports Hall of Fame.

finishing third in the latter year. From 1963 to 1966 Duke was the dominant team in the ACC, finishing first in the regular season race all four years, winning the conference tournament every year except 1965 (when North Carolina State, coached by Press Maravich, won in an upset), and advancing to the Final Four in 1963, 1964, and 1966. The 1963 team, led by national Player of the Year Art Heyman, finished third. The 1964 team, led by Olympian Jeff Mullins, advanced to the final game, during which it became the first of many teams to lose a championship game to UCLA. In 1966 the Blue Devils finished third, led by Bob Verga and Jack Marin.

Duke's Art Heyman, named an all-American in 1961, 1962, and 1963 and national Player of the Year in 1963, was instrumental in Duke's impressive third-place finish in the NCAA basketball tournament in the latter year. Heyman remains Duke's all-time leading scorer. Photograph supplied by the North Carolina Sports Hall of Fame.

UNC's basketball fortunes had revived by the middle 1960s. McGuire was replaced by Dean Smith, a relatively unknown UNC assistant. Smith won only eight games during his first year and was even hanged in effigy. Carolina recovered quickly, however, winning fifteen games in 1963 and 1965. Those teams were led by Billy Cunningham, an outstanding leaper nicknamed "the Kangaroo Kid." By 1967 Smith had recruited a succession of prep stars including Bob Lewis, Larry Miller, Dick Grubar, and Rusty Clark and was ready to challenge Bubas for ACC supremacy. In an unprecedented three-year run UNC finished first in the regular season, won the post-season ACC tournament, and advanced to the Final Four in 1967, 1968, and 1969. Miller was ACC Player of the Year in both 1967 and 1968. In 1968 Carolina advanced to the NCAA finals before losing handily to a UCLA powerhouse.

Carolina's 1969 post-season run was led by all-American Charlie Scott, who scored 40 points in the ACC tournament final victory over Duke and hit a last-second shot to beat Davidson 87-85 in the Eastern Regional

Leading the North Carolina Tar Heel basketball teams of the mid-1960s was Billy Cunningham (left), here shown in the uniform of the Carolina Cougars, the professional team for which he played in the late 1960s and early 1970s. Photograph courtesy Woody Gibson; supplied by the North Carolina Sports Hall of Fame.

final. Scott was not simply another in a long line of standout Tar Heel basketball players, however. Rather, he was the ACC's first black superstar. Prior to the racial integration of colleges and universities, such black North Carolinians as Walt Bellamy (New Bern), Happy Hairston (Winston-Salem), and Lou Hudson (Greensboro) were forced to go north. The absence of black players put southern schools at a competitive disadvantage, a fact made abundantly clear in 1963 when a Loyola of Chicago team starting four black players defeated all-white Duke in the Final Four. In 1965 Maryland became the first school in the ACC to have black players. In the 1966-1967 season Duke's C. B. Claiborne became the first black in the Big Four. UNC, Wake Forest, Davidson, and North Carolina State followed in short order. UNC's Scott and Davidson's Mike Maloy were stars by 1968, while in 1971 Charlie Davis of Wake Forest became the first black to win the ACC Player of the Year award.

Although racial integration in the state was accomplished fairly smoothly when compared to some states in the Deep South, it was not without some incidents. In 1965 UCLA's black players were subjected to racial harassment during a visit to North Carolina. When Charlie Scott finished second in the voting for ACC Player of the Year to South Carolina's John Roche in 1969 and 1970 he charged racial discrimination in the voting.

The successes of the highly publicized ACC tended to overshadow other college basketball in the state. The Big Four did receive one serious in-state challenge in the 1960s, however. In 1960 Charles (Lefty) Driesell was named head coach at Davidson College, a small, academically elite private school that was not accustomed to a position among the nation's college basketball elite. Yet Driesell, a tireless recruiter, was able to bring such stars as Terry Holland, Fred Hetzel, Dick Snyder, Mike Maloy, and Doug Cook to the small Davidson campus. In 1964 and 1965 Davidson had consecutive records of 22-4 and 24-2. Both of these superb seasons ended in bitter disappointment, however, as Davidson was upset in the Southern Conference tournament and was unable to compete in the NCAA tournament. In 1968 and 1969, however, Davidson won the tournament and advanced to the Eastern Regional finals, where it lost close games both years to UNC. The day after the 1969 NCAA loss Driesell announced that he was leaving Davidson for the head coaching job at the University of Maryland.

Other fine players and teams toiled in relative obscurity in the Carolinas Conference, the Mid-East Athletic Conference (MEAC), and the CIAA. In 1963 Western Carolina, coached by Jim Gudger and led by Mel Gibson, advanced to the NAIA championship game, where the Catamounts lost to Pan American. From 1965 through 1968 Western's Henry Logan, a guard, became a rare four-time NAIA all-American. High Point's Gene Littles and Guilford's Bob Kaufmann also had standout NAIA careers in the late 1960s before joining the pros. Prior to racial integration, the state's predominantly black schools turned out such stars as Sam Jones (North Carolina College), Al Attles (North Carolina A&T), Cleo Hill (Winston-Salem State), and Lee Davis (North Carolina College). Coaches like John McLendon at North Carolina Central, Cal Irvin at A&T, and Clarence (Bighouse) Gaines at Winston-Salem State established black powerhouses. In 1967 Winston-Salem State won the NCAA Division II national championship, led by a spectacular, high-scoring (41.5 points per game) guard, Earl (The Pearl) Monroe.

During a twenty-year tenure as head basketball coach at North Carolina A&T State University in Greensboro, Cal Irvin led his teams to more than 400 victories. Photograph supplied by the North Carolina Sports Hall of Fame.

The four North Carolina teams dominated the first fifteen years of the ACC. During this period no non-Big Four team finished the regular season higher than third and only Maryland in 1958 won the tournament. This began to change by the late 1960s. Frank McGuire returned to the league at South Carolina and made that program a national power before its departure from the ACC following the 1971 season. In the early 1970s Lefty Driesell did the same at Maryland, while Virginia and Clemson upgraded their programs. Georgia Tech joined the league for the 1979-1980 season and after a few lean years became competitive under the coaching of Bobby Cremins in the middle 1980s.

Yet, despite these challenges, the Big Four has continued to outperform the competition. UNC, for example, has appeared in the NCAA tournament every year since 1974. The architect of this success has been Dean Smith, who garnered national attention as one of America's most respected and innovative coaches, a reputation solidified in 1976 when he coached the United States team to an Olympic gold medal. A roll call of Smith's all-Americans in the 1970s would include North Carolina natives Robert McAdoo (Greensboro), Bobby Jones (Charlotte), Walter Davis (Pineville), and Phil Ford (Rocky Mount), along with Dennis Wuycik, Mitch Kupchak, and Mike O'Koren. UNC won the National Invitational Tournament (NIT) in 1971, while the 1972 Tar Heels, led by McAdoo and Wuycik, finished third in the NCAA. The 1977 team made the championship game despite a devastating run of injuries, only to fall victim to an emotional Marquette team.

If anything, UNC's program has become more successful in the 1980s. Smith's well-oiled recruiting network has brought such prep stars as Al Wood, James Worthy (Gastonia), Sam Perkins, Michael Jordan (Wilmington), Brad Daughtery (Swannanoa), Joe Wolf, Kenny Smith, Jeff Lebo, and J. R. Reid into the program. In 1981 the Tar Heels lost in the NCAA finals to Indiana, Smith's sixth unsuccessful trip to the Final Four. Smith's

Dean Smith, head basketball coach at UNC since 1961, has enjoyed unprecedented success by having his teams compete in every NCAA tournament since 1974. Smith's 1981-1982 team, led by freshman Michael Jordan, won the NCAA national championship. Photograph courtesy Office of Sports Information, UNC-CH.

fortunes improved the following year as Carolina defeated Georgetown 63-62 on a last-second jump shot by Michael Jordan. UNC ended that season with an extraordinary record of 32-2. Despite outstanding teams, UNC has not won an ACC tournament or returned to the Final Four since its 1982 championship. Its biggest post-season disappointment was a top-ranked 1984 team, led by all-Americans Jordan and Perkins, which was upset by Indiana in an early-round NCAA game. UNC lost in regional finals in 1983, 1985, 1987, and 1988. In 1986 UNC opened the palatial Smith Center, one of the largest on-campus basketball facilities in the United States.

North Carolina State's program reached a nadir during 1967, Norm Sloan's first year, when the team went 7-19. Sloan turned the program around quickly, however. By 1970 State was good enough to upset South Carolina and win the ACC tournament. In 1972 7 foot 4 inch center Tommy Burleson, a native of Avery County, arrived on the State varsity. He was joined the following year by Shelby's David Thompson and diminutive guard Monte Towe. The arrival of Thompson, a stunning player with exceptional leaping and shooting ability, was controversial. State was found guilty of violations in recruiting Thompson and was placed on probation in 1973. Thus, an undefeated 27-0 team was unable to go on to post-season play. The following year State rebounded from an early-season loss to UCLA to finish the regular season ranked number one in the nation. State advanced to post-season play by the narrowest of margins, a pulsating 103-100 overtime victory over Maryland in the ACC championship finals. This game, which has achieved an almost mythical

North Carolina State's exceptional David Thompson (No. 44) of Shelby, in combination with talented teammates, powered the Wolfpack to an NCAA tournament victory in 1974. Thompson was named an all-American in 1973, 1974, and 1975 and was national Player of the Year in 1974 and 1975. Photograph courtesy Wolfpack Sports Information, NCSU.

status, led to a new NCAA rule the following year that for the first time permitted two teams from the same conference to advance to the NCAA tournament. State made it to the Final Four, held that year in Greensboro, where it avenged its only loss of the season with a double-overtime 80-77 victory over UCLA. This ended UCLA's remarkable run of seven consecutive national championships. State ended its 30-1 season with an almost anticlimactic 76-64 victory over Marquette for the national title.

Although Thompson averaged 30 points per game in 1975, State was unable to overcome the loss of Burleson and repeat as ACC champs. The Wolfpack continued to be competitive through the 1970s through the efforts of all-conference players such as Kenny Carr and Charles (Hawkeye) Whitney. After the 1980 season, Sloan left State to become head coach at the University of Florida. He was replaced by little-known Jim Valvano, hired away from Iona College.

State's brief appearance in the 1982 NCAA tournament was a prelude to a remarkable 1983 tournament. In 1983 the Wolfpack was a good team that peaked at the right time. Led by an outstanding guard tandem of Sidney Lowe and Derek Whittenberg and smooth forward Thurl Bailey, State tied for third in the regular season that year. State caught fire in the ACC tournament, winning close games against Wake Forest, UNC, and Virginia to become conference champions. In the NCAA tournament the "Cardiac Pack" won a succession of heart-stopping victories, including another win over Virginia and its star player, Ralph Sampson. In the NCAA finals the Wolfpack defeated favored Houston 54-52 on Lorenzo Charles's last-second rebound dunk, capping a miracle national championship.

State has remained a power since the national championship year despite some off-court problems, the most publicized of which was Chris Washburn's campus break-in that caused him to miss most of the 1984-1985 season. Washburn returned to the Wolfpack for the 1985-1986 season and helped State advance to the finals of the Midwest Regionals. In 1987 State redeemed a mediocre regular season with an upset victory in the ACC tournament. The Wolfpack lost its NCAA openers in both 1987 and 1988.

After the 1969 season Vic Bubas left the Duke coaching slot to take a position in administration. His replacement, Bucky Waters, coached Duke into the NIT in 1970 and 1971 before the program began to decline. Hampered by continual player defections, Duke had a 12-14 season in 1973, its first losing season since 1939. Waters left shortly before the start of the 1973-1974 season. The Blue Devils then went 10-16 under interim coach Neil McGeachy. Bill Foster was hired from Utah for the 1975 season. Although Foster's first three teams were mediocre, he did reestablish Duke's national recruiting network. Blue Devils Jim Spanarkel, Mike Gminski (tied with Whitney), and Gene Banks were successive ACC Freshmen of the Year in 1976, 1977, and 1978. In 1978 the trio led Duke back into the national spotlight in a big way. A young Blue Devil team won the ACC tournament, the Eastern Regionals, and a Final Four match over Notre Dame to advance to the national championship game against heavily favored Kentucky. The Wildcats' Jack Givens scored a remarkable 41 points as Duke succumbed 94-88. Duke was ranked number one during much of the next two seasons as Spanarkel and Gminski achieved all-American status, but the Blue Devils were unable to return to the Final Four—although the 1980 team fell only one game short.

Foster left Duke for South Carolina after the 1980 season. His surprise replacement was little-known Army coach Mike Krzyzewski, whose first three seasons resulted in a combined 38-47 record and some grumbling among the Blue Devil faithful. But Duke's 11-17 1983 team contained the seeds of future successes—a freshman class of Johnny Dawkins, Mark Alarie, David Henderson, and Jay Bilas. Led by this class, Duke returned to the NCAA tournament with twenty-plus wins in 1984 and 1985. In 1986, with Dawkins a unanimous all-American, Duke won an NCAA record thirty-seven games, finished first in the ACC regular season, won the ACC tournament, entered the NCAA tournament ranked number one, and advanced to the championship game. The Blue Devils led Louisville for most of a close game before losing their shooting touch and a 72-69 heartbreaker. Despite the loss of four starters, Duke returned to the NCAA final sixteen in 1987. In 1988, led by league Player of the Year Danny Ferry, the Blue Devils won the ACC tournament and advanced to the Final Four, where they lost to eventual national champion Kansas.

Wake Forest has been somewhat less successful than its Big Four rivals in the 1970s and 1980s. Under Carl Tacy the Deacons made NCAA appearances in 1977, 1981, 1982, and 1984. Wake Forest advanced to regional finals in 1977 and 1984 before losing respectively to Marquette and Houston. In 1983 Wake Forest advanced to the NIT semifinals. Among the better Wake Forest players of the Tacy era were Skip Brown, Rod Griffin, Frank Johnson, Danny Young, and Kenny Green. Tacy left after the 1985 season. His replacement, Bob Staak, has been plagued by injuries and player transfers and has had trouble rebuilding the program. Wake's dismal 1986 and 1987 seasons were partially redeemed by superquick 5 foot 3 inch fan favorite Tyrone (Mugsy) Bogues, whose ball-handling and defensive skills led to an all-conference designation in 1987.

The popularity of the ACC continued to obscure other basketball in the state in the 1970s and 1980s. The most successful challenge to Big Four hegemony in the state came from UNC-Charlotte in the mid-1970s. Led by Kinston native Cedric (Cornbread) Maxwell, UNCC finished as NIT runner-up in 1976 and was a surprise visitor to the Final Four in 1977, where it lost a last-second decision to eventual champion Marquette. UNCC was unable to sustain this level of success, however. Following a precipitous decline in the early 1980s, the 49ers, by then a member of the sprawling Sun Belt Conference, began to rebound under the coaching tenure of former Duke all-American and NBA all-star Jeff Mullins.

Davidson College, UNCC's Mecklenburg County neighbor, likewise has been unable to sustain its highest level of success. Lefty Driesell left Davidson for Maryland at the close of the 1969 season. His replacement, Terry Holland, kept the program successful through 1974, when he accepted the head coaching position at the University of Virginia. Since that time a succession of coaches has generally kept Davidson competitive within the Southern Conference but not on the national level attained by Driesell in the 1960s. Davidson left the Southern Conference at the conclusion of the 1988 season. Appalachian State and Western Carolina, the other North Carolina schools in the Southern Conference, have usually occupied a position in the middle of the league, although Appalachian State had a brief period of success in the late 1970s in the brief coaching tenure there of Bobby Cremins.

Other basketball programs in the state have upgraded to Division I status, the highest NCAA level, in recent years. After a brief period in the Southern Conference, East Carolina is now a member of the Colonial Conference, as is UNC-Wilmington. Campbell University and UNC-Asheville are members of the recently formed Big South Conference. North Carolina A&T, coached by Don Corbett, has dominated the Mid-East Athletic Conference in recent years, winning the post-season tournament and advancing to the NCAA every year from 1982 through 1988. The Aggies have yet to win an NCAA tournament game, however.

Other schools have prospered in the smaller environs of the NAIA. Many of these schools, such as Atlantic Christian College, North Carolina Wesleyan, and Methodist College, do not have football programs and rely on their basketball teams for athletic visibility. The state has produced one NAIA champion in recent years. In 1973 Guilford College won the title under the leadership of future NBA stars Lloyd (World) Free and M. L. Carr. Campbell, prior to its entry into Division I, was NAIA runner-up in 1977, while St. Augustine's was NCAA Division II runner-up in 1984. At Winston-Salem State, Bighouse Gaines has quietly compiled a spectacular record. At the end of the 1988 season Gaines was the winningest active coach in the NCAA.

Given the basketball success of North Carolina colleges in the 1940s and 1950s, it is surprising that area collegians had little impact on the pro scene in this period. In the pre-expansion era the eight-team NBA had few roster spots, and the league was dominated by college players from the East and Midwest. Area stars such as Lennie Rosenbluth, Pete Brennan, Ronnie Shavlik, Sammy Ranzino, and Dickie Hemric had brief, unexceptional pro careers. Dick Groat played one year in the NBA before

Winston-Salem State University's head basketball coach Clarence (Bighouse) Gaines was the winningest active coach in the NCAA at the end of 1988 . His 1966-1967 team, led by guard Earl (The Pearl) Monroe, won the NCAA Division II national championship. Photograph supplied by the North Carolina Sports Hall of Fame.

concentrating on his baseball career. Bones McKinney, George Glamack, and Belus Smawley of Appalachian State were the most successful area players in the 1940s and 1950s.

With the basketball is Sam Jones, standout at North Carolina College (now North Carolina Central University) who later played for the NBA's Boston Celtics for twelve years. Photograph supplied by the North Carolina Sports Hall of Fame.

North Carolina players began to make more of an impact in the 1960s, a decade during which the league expanded from eight to fourteen teams. Sam Jones of North Carolina Central, Lee Shaffer and Billy Cunningham of UNC, Jeff Mullins and Jack Marin of Duke, and Earl Monroe of Winston-Salem State were perennial all-stars in the 1960s and early 1970s. North Carolina natives Walt Bellamy and Lou Hudson were likewise members of the NBA's elite, as was former Raleigh high school star Pete Maravich.

Not surprisingly, numerous former UNC players have been standouts in the NBA in the 1970s and 1980s. Four former Tar Heels—Robert McAdoo in 1973, Walter Davis in 1978, Phil Ford in 1979, and Michael Jordan in 1985—were named NBA Rookies of the Year. McAdoo in 1975 and Jordan in 1988 won the league's Most Valuable Player award, while both have led the league in scoring. Charlie Scott, Bobby Jones, James Worthy, and Sam Perkins are among other former UNC players to achieve NBA success. David Thompson made several NBA all-star teams, as did Lloyd Free of Guilford and John Drew of Gardner-Webb. Other top NBA players of this period with North Carolina college connections include Mike Gminski, Gene Banks, and Johnny Dawkins of Duke; Kenny Carr, Thurl Bailey, and Nate MacMillan of North Carolina State; Frank Johnson of Wake Forest; and Cornbread Maxwell of UNC-Charlotte. The most spectacular NBA career has been that of the marvelously gifted "Air" Jordan, who by the late 1980s had become one of the best-known and highest-paid athletes in the world. In the 1986-1987 season Jordan averaged 37.1 points per game, the highest average ever for an NBA guard. He repeated as the league's leading scorer in 1987-1988.

One of the best-known and highest-paid athletes in the world is Wilmington native Michael Jordan, who, following a spectacular career at UNC, has excelled as a guard for the NBA's Chicago Bulls. Jordan's consistent scoring abilities rank him as one of the nation's leading celebrities in the sports world. Photograph courtesy Office of Sports Information, UNC-CH.

In 1967 the American Basketball Association challenged the NBA. From its inception the ABA featured a generous helping of North Carolina players, such as Doug Moe and Larry Brown from UNC, Bob Verga and Art Heyman from Duke, and Gene Littles from High Point College. After the 1969 season the Houston Mavericks franchise moved to North Carolina and became the Carolina Cougars. The Cougars took the unusual step of dividing their games among the state's three largest cities— Charlotte, Greensboro, and Raleigh. They also relied heavily on familiar names, such as their first coach, Bones McKinney, and former area college players such as Bob Verga and Larry Miller (UNC). The Cougars were 42-42 in their first year as Verga finished second in the league scoring race with a 27.5 average, but two consecutive losing seasons followed.

The next year, the 1972-1973 season, the Cougars had a new coach, Larry Brown, and new players Billy Cunningham, Mack Calvin, and Tom Owens, who led the team to a regular-season record of 57-27, the best in the league. Cunningham was the league MVP and finished in the ABA top ten in scoring, rebounds, and assists. The Cougars lost a hard-fought seven-game series to the Kentucky Colonels in the Eastern finals. That series marked the high-water mark for the Cougars. The following season Cunningham was lost with a kidney ailment. Minus their star the Cougars slumped to 47-37, third place in the Eastern Division, and a first-round playoff loss. The franchise was then moved to St. Louis, where it folded after two lackluster seasons.

While Everett Case, Frank McGuire, and others were making North Carolina synonymous with college basketball, the sport was still largely an intramural activity for college women. Some women were able to find competitive outlets in YWCA or industrial leagues. Hanes Hosiery of Winston-Salem sponsored an early 1950s dynasty. Coached by Virgil Yow and led by Eunies Futch and Eckie Jordan, the Hanes Hosiery team won the AAU national championship in 1951, 1952, and 1953. A loss in the 1954 championship game ended a 104-game winning streak. Hanes dropped its sponsorship shortly afterward, and the team was disbanded.

By the early 1970s UNC and East Carolina were among the schools fielding women's basketball teams. It took the passage of Title IX of the 1972 Education Amendment Act to institute high-level full-scholarship basketball for women. The ACC held its first women's tournament in 1978. The increasingly fast-paced women's game has gained increased media attention and fan support through the 1980s, becoming the most visible women's sport on most campuses.

In the fall of 1975 Kay Yow left Elon College to become the head coach of the North Carolina State women's team. Yow recruited and developed such stars as Genia Beasley, Linda (Hawkeye) Page, and Trudi Lacey and turned State into the dominant team in the area. Yow was an assistant for the 1984 United States Women's Olympic team, coached the United

Kay Yow has served as women's basketball coach at North Carolina State University since 1975. In addition to achieving an enviable record of wins for the Lady Wolfpack, Ms. Yow has excelled as a coach in international competition, particularly the Olympics. Photograph courtesy Wolfpack Sports Information, NCSU.

States to a gold medal in the 1986 World Championships, and coached the United States Women's Olympic team to the Olympic Gold Medal in 1988. East Carolina University was also a power in the 1970s under the coaching of Catherine Bolton and then Cathy Andruzzi. In many of these years ECU was State's primary challenger for in-state supremacy. High Point College won the AIAW Division II championship in 1976.

In the 1980s the women's scene in the state has become more competitive. UNC, Duke, and Wake Forest have upgraded their programs in response to State's dominance. Each has appeared in post-season tournaments, while players such as Chris Moreland of Duke and Amy Privette of Wake Forest have garnered attention for their skills. Although women's college basketball receives far less attention than men's basketball in the area, special promotions have led to some impressive crowds and set the stage for further growth.

Since the end of World War II golf has become almost as identified with North Carolina as college basketball. Synonymous with golf in the state is the Greater Greensboro Open. The GGO resumed play in 1945 and has been an annual fixture on the professional golf tour ever since. The tournament was dominated in its early years by Sam Snead, who won it an astounding eight times between 1938 and 1965. In addition to Snead, leading golfers who have won the GGO over the years include Mike Souchak, Billy Casper, Doug Sanders, Julius Boros, Gene Littler, Gary Player, Chi Chi Rodriguez, Tom Weiskopf, Larry Nelson, Joey Sindelar, and Sandy Lyle. Other professional tournaments in the state have come and gone. Charlotte hosted the Charlotte Open until 1948 and the Kemper Open from 1968 until it moved to Washington, D.C., in 1979. The Azalea Open was held in Wilmington from 1949 until 1971, while

Pinehurst has hosted several pro tourneys, including the World Open. Pinehurst is now the home of the World Golf Hall of Fame.

North Carolina has produced more than its share of outstanding pro golfers. Clayton Heafner of Charlotte was an outstanding player in the 1940s and early 1950s, while his son Vance played on the PGA tour in the 1980s. Fayetteville's Raymond Floyd is perhaps the best player produced in North Carolina. He has won more than twenty professional tournaments, including the 1969 PGA, the 1976 Masters, the 1982 PGA, and the 1986 United States Open. Scott Hoch of Raleigh, Joe Inman of Greensboro, Chip Beck of Fayetteville, and Clarence Rose of Goldsboro are among other top Tar Heel players. Charlie Sifford of Charlotte started as a caddy and fought years of racial discrimination to become the first black to win a PGA tournament. Roxboro's Jim Thorpe is one of the top black players on the 1980s PGA tour.

One of North Carolina's premier professional golfers is Raymond Floyd of Fayetteville, winner of more than twenty PGA-sanctioned tournaments, including two PGAs, one Masters, and one U.S. Open. Photograph courtesy World Golf Hall of Fame, Pinehurst.

Other North Carolina golfers have been successful in the amateur ranks. Billy Joe Patton, Bill Harvey, Dale Morey, and Harvie Ward all had outstanding amateur careers. Ward, a Tarboro native, won the NCAA championship in 1949 while at UNC and numerous national and international tournaments throughout the 1960s. Patton, a Morganton native, was an outstanding amateur in the 1950s and shocked the golfing world in 1954 when he almost won the prestigious Masters, losing by only a single stroke.

Ward was only one of a growing number of outstanding college golfers in the state. Mike Souchak and Art Wall were standout golfers at Duke before moving on to illustrious careers in the PGA. The charismatic Arnold Palmer, who played at Wake Forest and was the first ACC champion in 1954, later joined the PGA tour and led it to new heights of

While a student at Wake Forest University, Arnold Palmer won the Atlantic Coast Conference's first championship in 1954. He went on to become the most popular professional golfer of his time. Photograph courtesy Office of Sports Information, Wake Forest University.

popularity while becoming the most popular golfer of his time. Palmer was the harbinger of what would become a major college golf dynasty. Under the tutelage of coach Jesse Haddock, Wake Forest has dominated ACC golf since the middle 1960s and has won NCAA titles in 1974, 1975, and 1986. Haddock's all-Americans have included Jack Lewis, Lanny Wadkins, Curtis Strange, Joe Inman, Gary Hallberg, Jay Haas, and Chris Kite. Strange in 1974, Haas in 1975, and Hallberg in 1979 all won the NCAA tournament individual crown, as did UNC's John Inman in 1984. Wadkins won the PGA championship in 1977. In 1988 Strange established himself as one of the world's premier golfers when he won the United States Open championship and became the first golfer to win more than one million dollars in a single year.

The state has not been as successful producing women golfers. Estelle Lawson Page of Chapel Hill continued her amateur career through the 1940s, while adopted Tar Heel Peggy Kirk Bell, a native of Ohio who moved to Southern Pines in 1951, played on the LPGA tour in the 1950s. Carol Mann attended UNC-Greensboro in the late 1950s before leaving and becoming a dominant player on the LPGA tour in the 1960s. Kinston's Donna White has had some success on the women's circuit in the 1980s. Several LPGA tournaments have come and gone, leaving the Henredon Classic in High Point as the sole women's pro tourney in North Carolina. In 1988 the Henredon became the Pat Bradley Tournament. In recent years women's college golf has become a fixture in the state. The Duke women's team has had the most successful program, with several NCAA top-ten finishes.

Although the pro tennis tour has made occasional stops in North Carolina, there is no tennis equivalent of the GGO. A number of college players in the state have made an impact on the sport. Vic Seixas starred at UNC before and after World War II with a stint in the Air Force in between. After graduating from UNC in 1949, Seixas won Wimbledon in 1953 and the United States Open championship in 1954 and captained the United States Davis Cup team in 1952 and 1964. UNC continued to boast the dominant tennis program in the state until the middle 1970s. Under the coaching of Don Skakle, the Tar Heels won or shared twenty-two of the first twenty-five ACC tennis championships. Tar Heel Freddie McNair was a three-time all-American in the early 1970s. Following Skakle's death in 1980, UNC's position of dominance eroded, while other programs improved. Charlotte and North Carolina State's John Sadri advanced to the NCAA championship in 1978, losing in a memorable final to Stanford's John McEnroe. Duke has produced a series of top-twenty programs in the 1980s featuring such stars as Marc Flur and Jeff Hersh. Sadri, Shelby's Tim Wilkinson, and Asheville's Lawson Duncan (who played collegiately at Clemson) have all had some success on the pro tennis circuit.

The outstanding college female tennis player is Laura Dupont of Charlotte, who dominated the area college scene in the early 1970s at UNC before joining the pro circuit. Dupont played at a time when women's tennis was not yet an official ACC sport. Indeed, the first ACC women's tennis championship wasn't held until 1978. Clemson has dominated the league, although Duke won the 1988 championship.

Like tennis, track and field in the state has largely been associated with colleges and universities. The Olympics have long been the pinnacle of achievement for track and field athletes, and several North Carolinians have excelled at that level. The versatile Floyd (Chunk) Simmons entered UNC after seeing combat in World War II. Upon finishing at Carolina, Simmons continued running for the Los Angeles Athletic Club and won bronze medals in the decathlon in both the 1948 and 1952 Olympics. In 1955 Dave Sime of Duke set or equaled world records in the 220-yard low hurdles, the 220-yard dash, and the 100-yard dash. He ran the world's first 20.0-second 220-yard dash on June 3, 1955, at the AAU championship meet in Stockton, California. Regarded as the world's fastest human, Sime was unable to qualify for the 1956 Olympic team because of an injury. That same year the more fortunate Lee Calhoun of North Carolina Central won the 110-meter high hurdles at the Olympics, while Duke's Joel Shankle finished third. Calhoun repeated his gold-medal performance in 1960, making him the first man to win two gold medals in that event. Sime made the 1960 Olympic team and finished a close second in the 100-meter final. His last chance to win Olympic gold ended when the United States 4x100-meter relay team was disqualified for a lane violation after an apparent victory.

Jim Beatty, a 1957 UNC graduate, made the 1960 Olympic team at 5,000 meters but, hampered by an injured foot, finished far back. In 1962

Track star Jim Beatty, a graduate of UNC, in 1962 became the first runner in the world to break the four-minute mile in indoor competition. This feat won for him the 1962 Sullivan Award, which recognizes the nation's best amateur athlete. Photograph from the files of the Division of Archives and History.

at Los Angeles Beatty ran the world's first indoor sub-four-minute mile, with a 3:58.9 performance. That year Beatty won the Sullivan Award as the nation's best amateur athlete. In the 1972 Munich Olympics Vince Matthews of Johnson C. Smith University won the 400 meters, while Larry Black of North Carolina Central finished second in the 200 meters. Tony Waldrop of Columbus, North Carolina, and UNC ran a world indoor record mile of 3:55.0 in 1974, one of a series of superb runs that enabled him to win the McKelvin Award as the ACC's top athlete that year, defeating among others North Carolina State basketball star David Thompson.

One of the outstanding figures in American track and field during this period was North Carolina Central head coach Leroy Walker. In addition to coaching a number of Olympic medalists and scores of college stars, Walker was head coach of the highly successful 1976 United States men's Olympic team. Duke coach Al Buehler was also involved with several Olympic teams as a coach or manager. In recent years North Carolina State has dominated the ACC, winning the conference championship from 1982 through 1988. State has produced a series of outstanding sprinters, including the 1985 NCAA champion 4x100-meter relay team of Auguston Young, Alston Glenn, Danny Peebles, and Harvey McSwain. East Carolina sprinter Lee Vernon McNeil made the 1988 United States Olympic team in the 4x100-meter relay. McNeil suffered an unfortunate Olympics, however, as he was involved in a botched baton pass that elimi-nated the United States team in a preliminary round.

North Carolina has also produced some standout women track stars. Kathy McMillan of Raeford finished second in the 1976 Olympic long jump. The North Carolina State women's cross-country team has been a national power since the late 1970s. The State women won the 1979 and

North Carolina Central University track and field coach Leroy Walker is perhaps best known for his extensive involvement in training programs aimed at improving the performance of America's participants in Olympic competitions. Walker served with distinction as head coach of the 1976 United States men's Olympic track and field team. Photograph supplied by the North Carolina Sports Hall of Fame.

Kathy McMillan of Raeford won a silver medal in the 1976 Olympics with a long jump of 21 feet 10¼ inches. Photograph courtesy the *News and Observer* (Raleigh); supplied by the North Carolina Sports Hall of Fame.

1980 AIAW national championships after finishing second in 1978. They have since finished in the top three in the NCAA championships in 1983, 1984, 1985, and 1987. Over the years this team has featured such stars as Julie Shea, Mary Shea, Betty Springs (Geiger), Suzie Tuffey, and, for a brief period, Joan Benoit. Julie Shea was AIAW individual cross-country champion in 1979 and 1980 and was a four-time cross-country all-American. Springs was also a four-time all-American and won the individual NCAA title in 1981 and 1983. Tuffey was NCAA champion in 1985. These distance runners have also served as the nucleus of State's women track teams and have won numerous individual all-American honors. Julie Shea became the first woman to win the McKelvin Award

Sisters Mary (left) and Julie Shea excelled at cross-country distance running while they were in school together at North Carolina State. Julie Shea was twice named AIAW individual cross-country champion and was four times a cross-country all-American. Photograph courtesy Wolfpack Sports Information, NCSU.

in 1980. She repeated in 1981, and that same year also won the Broderick Cup as the outstanding female college athlete in the United States. Ellison Goodhall and Ellen Reynolds of Duke, Joan Nesbit of UNC, and Karen Dunn of Wake Forest are among other outstanding women distance runners produced in the state.

International track and field came to North Carolina in 1971 when Duke hosted a dual meet between the national team of the United States and a Pan-African team that represented a number of African countries. Duke University hosted the Martin Luther King Games in 1973, a United States-USSR dual meet in 1974, and a triple meet entered by the United States, West Germany, and Pan Africa in 1975. Major invitational meets were held at Duke in 1979 and 1982. These meets benefited from the organizational skills of Duke coach Al Buehler and Leroy Walker and featured a galaxy of national and international stars.

Football and basketball are at the top of a college hierarchy that is delineated by their revenue-producing capacities. Indeed, other college sports are defined as nonrevenue sports. Baseball, by virtue of its tradition and history, and track and field, by virtue of its capacity to produce members of highly publicized teams that represent the United States in international competition, are relatively well publicized. College golf draws a measure of attention in the state because of the large number of area alumni, particularly from Wake Forest, active in the PGA. Other nonrevenue sports operate in relative isolation. These sports are rarely on television, are generally played before small crowds, and are buried on the back pages of the sports section if indeed they are recognized at all. Yet these sports all have their share of dedicated, skilled scholarship athletes, knowledgeable and innovative coaches, local dynasties, and a hard core of interested and knowledgeable fans.

In North Carolina the sport that has come closest to breaking out of this pattern is soccer. Indeed, in the 1980s North Carolina has become something of a hotbed of college soccer. Although the sport is far from financial self-sufficiency, several North Carolina colleges have built impressive new facilities, and paying crowds in the thousands are not uncommon. For a brief period in the late 1970s Appalachian State became a national power, largely with foreign-born players. In the 1980s Duke, UNC; and North Carolina State have become frequent denizens of the national top ten and frequent NCAA tournament participants. Under the coaching tutelage of John Rennie, Duke has produced a nationally prominent program. The Blue Devils advanced to the NCAA championship game in 1982, losing a 2-1 eight-overtime game to Indiana.

In the newly popular realm of soccer, Duke head coach John Rennie has built the Blue Devil teams of the 1980s into nationally recognized powers. Duke's 1986 defeat of the University of Akron was the university's first NCAA championship in any sport. Photograph courtesy Duke Sports Information.

In 1986 Duke defeated Akron 1-0 to post the school's first NCAA championship in any sport. Duke players Joe Ulrich (1982), Mike Jeffries (1983), Tom Kain (1985), and John Kerr (1986) have won the Hermann Award, presented to the nation's outstanding college player. Duke's successes pale compared to the triumphs of UNC-Greensboro, however. The Spartans have won the NCAA-Division III (nonscholarship) men's national championship in 1982, 1983, 1985, 1986, and 1987. UNC-Chapel Hill advanced to the NCAA final four in 1987.

Other sports such as wrestling, swimming, cross-country, fencing, and lacrosse have failed to achieve the spurt of popularity enjoyed by soccer. The success of North Carolina State's swimming program has paralleled that of the UNC tennis program. The Wolfpack won every ACC

Jubilant members of the UNC-G Spartans soccer team lift coach Michael Parker into the air after defeating Washington University to win the NCAA Division III men's soccer championship in St. Louis, Missouri, in 1985. The UNC-G soccer team won similar championships in 1982, 1983, 1986, and 1987. Photograph courtesy Department of Intercollegiate Athletics, UNC-G.

swimming championship from 1966 through 1982, with the exception of 1970. Among coach Willis Casey's Olympians was Steve Rerych, who won two gold medals in the 1968 Olympics. UNC's Thompson Mann won a gold medal in 1964 in the 400-meter medley relay. East Carolina won NAIA national championships in 1957 and 1959. Nancy Hogshead of Duke won three gold medals in the 1984 Olympics, while UNC's Sue Walsh captured ten national championships in the early 1980s. UNC has dominated women's swimming in the ACC, which held its first women's tournament in 1978. In wrestling both UNC and North Carolina State have had numerous top-twenty teams and have produced such occasional stars as UNC's C. D. Mock and State's Matt Reiss, 300-plus-pound heavyweight Tab Thacker, and Scott Taylor, all NCAA champions in the 1980s. The sport of lacrosse has been limited by the relatively few high schools producing college-caliber players. Only four ACC schools field lacrosse teams, largely because of difficulties recruiting players. UNC has had the most successful program, winning NCAA championships in 1981, 1982, and 1986.

If most men's nonrevenue sports have a difficult time competing with basketball and football, the same is doubly true for women's sports, all of which are essentially nonrevenue. Since the advent of Title IX, however, the number of women's sports and female scholarship athletes has increased dramatically. Women compete in basketball, track and field, soccer, cross-country, tennis, volleyball, swimming, and field hockey. The most successful college team of the 1980s is the UNC women's soccer team, winner of the AIAW national championship in 1981 and NCAA championships in 1982, 1983, 1984, 1986, 1987, and 1988. Tar Heel April

UNC star April Heinrichs is widely regarded as one of the most accomplished female soccer players in the United States. Photograph courtesy Office of Sports Information, UNC-CH.

Heinrichs is widely regarded as one of the finest female soccer players in the United States. Carolina's dominance has overshadowed several nationally ranked North Carolina State teams, including the 1988 NCAA runner-up.

The most popular nonscholastic sport in North Carolina is the quintessentially southern sport of stock-car racing. The origins of stock-car racing are firmly grounded in southern moonshine mythology, good ole boys, and breathtaking runs away from revenuers on dangerous rural roads on moonlit nights.

The image of hard-charging, hard-drinking hell raisers belies the fact that the National Association for Stock Car Auto Racing (NASCAR) has become a multimillion-dollar business. NASCAR was incorporated in 1948. The organization's first races featured heavily modified cars. The following year the young organization decided to try a new tactic, using new cars, at least theoretically right out of the showroom. The first "new car" race was held June 19, 1949, on a three-quarter-mile dirt track in Charlotte. Kansan Jim Roper won the race. This was the beginning of NASCAR's fabulously successful Grand National Division, which consists of late-model cars. NASCAR benefited from postwar prosperity, which generated previously unknown levels of interest in automobiles. By the middle 1950s the major automobile manufacturers were heavily involved in stock-car racing, investing time, money, and prestige in producing faster race cars.

Several of the early legends of NASCAR were North Carolinians. Junior Johnson of Ronda (Wilkes County) won more than fifty Grand National events and became a southern folk hero as a reconstructed

Two of the most influential and popular practitioners of stock-car racing under the auspices of NASCAR are North Carolinians Junior Johnson of Ronda (top) and Richard Petty of Level Cross (bottom). Both men are veteran competitors who have witnessed an evolution of the sport from a provincial backwater affair informally conducted on dirt tracks to a multimillion-dollar spectacular featuring consistently heavy attendance and a national following via the media. Both photographs from the files of the Division of Archives and History.

moonshiner. Buck Baker of Charlotte, Lee Petty of Level Cross, Herb Thomas of Olivia, Jim Paschal of High Point, and Speedy Thompson of Monroe were other early standouts. Latter stars include Richard Petty and Buddy Baker (both sons of early NASCAR stars), Ned Jarrett of Hickory, Benny Parsons of Wilkesboro, Dale Earnhardt of Kannapolis, and Bobby Isaac of Catawba County. Richard Petty, who won his first NASCAR race in 1960, has become the most successful racer in NASCAR history and one of the most popular athletes ever in North Carolina. "King Richard" entered the 1989 racing season with 200 career NASCAR Grand National victories, more than any other racer.

Through the years stock-car racing has evolved from small, dangerous tracks to modern super speedways such as those at Charlotte, Rockingham, and North Wilkesboro. The 1 1/2-mile Charlotte Motor Speedway was opened in 1961 and hosts the World 600 and the National 500 annually. Every Memorial Day weekend the World 600 attracts more than 100,000 people, the largest sporting crowds in North Carolina. Winners of the World 600 include the cream of NASCAR's crop, including David Pearson, Buddy Baker, Cale Yarborough, and Richard Petty. Charlotte's position of prominence in the stock-car racing world is further solidified by the large number of racing teams headquartered there. The one-mile-long North Carolina Motor Speedway outside Rockingham is the site of the Carolina 500 and the American 500. Smaller tracks, many of them dirt, dot the state, providing a minor league to the big league of NASCAR.

Boxing has rarely been a major spectator sport in North Carolina, or indeed much of the rest of the South. Much of the impetus for boxing in the Northeast and Midwest historically has come from immigrants, groups notably absent from North Carolina. Heavyweight champion Floyd Patterson was born in North Carolina but moved north at an early age. Likewise "Sugar Ray" Leonard moved from his birthplace of Wilmington at an early age. Professional boxing cards in the state generally have relied upon the presence of the rare local boxer of substance, such as Charlotte's Bernard Taylor and Kelvin Seabrooks, or Harnett County heavyweight James (Bonecrusher) Smith, who gained a brief share of the heavyweight championship in 1986 before a one-sided loss to Mike Tyson the following year. In recent years military bases at Fort Bragg and Camp Lejeune have become centers of amateur boxing, providing soldiers and marines for United States amateur boxing teams. Brothers Leon and Michael Spinks, both gold medal winners in the 1976 Olympics and later heavyweight champions, boxed at Camp Lejeune prior to their Olympic glory.

Another professional sport that has been little in evidence in North Carolina in recent years is horse racing. The absence of pari-mutuel gambling (where the bettors determine the odds) has made the state unattractive to big-time racing. Nonetheless, the state has an active horse-breeding industry and some races, most notably steeplechasing in Moore

County. In recent years the General Assembly has made several unsuccessful attempts to legalize pari-mutuel gambling in the state. Given the passage of similar bills in other southern states, it is not unlikely that some form of big-time horse racing will eventually become part of the North Carolina sporting scene.

Some sports have largely been participant activities in North Carolina. Since the 1940s bowling has been a popular participant sport, with an unusually large number of women. Some Tar Heels have made a mark on professional bowling, including Maxine Allen of Seaboard, George Pappas of Charlotte, and Tommy Tuttle of King. Softball, especially the slow-pitch variety, has also become a popular participant sport. The more difficult fast-pitch variety is less pervasive. Since the 1970s, running, bicycling, and swimming have become part of the life-styles of thousands of North Carolinians. Although some road races such as the mid-summer five-mile Moonlight Race in the mountain resort community of Maggie have attracted world-class runners, other races such as the *Charlotte Observer* Marathon and the Great Raleigh Road Race have largely featured thousands of recreational runners. Virtually every municipality has a parks and recreation department that encourages organized competition in a plethora of sports.

Hunting and fishing continue to occupy the leisure time of large numbers of Tar Heels, although neither is the universal activity it was in an earlier, more rural age. The North Carolina Wildlife Resources Commission, an evolution of the earlier State Game Commission, continues to manage wildlife in the state. Even skiing, a sport seemingly alien to the state, has made a recreational impact in the mountains as a result of the introduction of snow-making machinery in the early 1960s. Such resorts as Sugar Mountain and Ski Beech attract hundreds of thousands of skiers annually.

Unfortunately, sports pages in North Carolina in recent years have not been restricted to national championships teams, all-Americans, and Olympic berths. The Tar Heel sport scene is a microcosm of a larger sporting world that has been in constant turmoil throughout the 1980s. Numerous North Carolina athletes have had careers shortened and their lives adversely affected by abuse of drugs, both legal and illegal. Books such as Lawrence Taylor's *LT: Living on the Edge* detail a professional sports world in which casual drug use is almost epidemic. Illegal drugs, labor disputes, and agents have helped make the sports page resemble a series of legal briefs.

The relationship between colleges and sports has come under increased scrutiny in North Carolina and throughout the nation. Although North Carolina schools have escaped major recruiting scandals in the 1980s, several have come under criticism for low graduation rates, admission of marginal students, the excessive influence of booster and alumni organizations, drugs, and occasional brushes with the law. The state's colleges and universities have been part of a national discussion concerning the future of college athletics that has led to scholarship limitations, freshmen eligibility, the elimination of booster clubs in recruiting, the use of Scholastic Aptitude Test scores to determine eligibility, and limits on red-shirting. The extraordinary amount of money being funneled into college athletic programs is a continuing source of concern for college administrators seeking to control athletic programs. The fact that thoughtful North Carolina university and athletic officials, like their counterparts throughout the nation, disagree on such basic concerns as freshmen eligibility and standardized admission regulations suggests that this discussion will continue for years to come.

The future of college athletics is only a part of the future of North Carolina sports. Two sporting events in the late 1980s may presage a change in North Carolina's position in the sporting world. In the summer of 1987 the communities of Raleigh, Durham, Chapel Hill, Cary, and Greensboro combined to host the multisport United States Olympic Festival. Old favorites such as basketball, baseball, and soccer were mixed with sports not often seen at a high competitive level in North Carolina, such as figure skating, ice hockey, and gymnastics. Attendance records were set in numerous events, while a wide variety of sporting venues were displayed to amateur sports officials throughout the nation. The fallout from the Olympic Festival will likely include an increasing number of national and even international amateur sporting events in the state.

In the fall of 1988 the Charlotte Hornets began play in the National Basketball Association. Charlotte has had other pro franchises such as the Carolina Cougars (shared with Greensboro and Raleigh) of the ABA, the Carolina Lightning of the American Soccer League, the Charlotte Hornets of the World Football League, and the Charlotte Checkers of the Eastern Hockey League. None of these leagues, however, were at the top of their respective pecking orders. The NBA Hornets are the first top-level pro sports team in the state. Charlotte sports fans greeted the arrival of the NBA with predictions of future franchises in the NFL and major league baseball. It remains to be seen whether pro sports will supplant North Carolina's traditional love affair with college sports.

Selected Bibliography

Space limitations prohibit a comprehensive listing of sources consulted. The histories of numerous counties, cities, colleges, and universities; a number of general histories of sport; and articles in contemporary newspapers have been purposely omitted.

Books

Barrier, Smith. *On Carolina's Gridiron, 1888-1936: A History of Football at the University of North Carolina*. Durham: Seeman Printery, 1937.

_____. *On Tobacco Road: Basketball in North Carolina*. New York: Leisure Press, 1983.

Beezley, Bill. *The Wolfpack: Intercollegiate Athletics at North Carolina State University*. Raleigh: North Carolina State University, 1976.

Blanchard, Elizabeth Amis Cameron, and Manly Wade Wellman. *The Life and Times of Sir Archie: The Story of America's Greatest Thoroughbred, 1805-1833*. Chapel Hill: University of North Carolina Press, 1958.

Brill, Bill. *Duke Basketball: An Illustrated History*. Dallas, Texas: Taylor Publishing Company, 1986.

Carlyle, Lewis. *North Carolina Tennis History*. Raleigh: North Carolina Tennis Association, 1978.

Chrisman, David F. *The History of the Piedmont League (1920-1955)*. Bend, Oregon: Maverick Publishers, 1986.

Corrie, Bruce A. *The Atlantic Coast Conference, 1953-1978*. Durham: Carolina Academic Press, 1978.

Elliott, William. *Carolina Sports by Land and Water*. Columbia, South Carolina: The State Company, Printers, 1978.

Harville, Charlie. *Sports in North Carolina: A Photographic History*. Norfolk: Donning Company, 1977.

Johnson, Guion Griffis. *Ante-Bellum North Carolina: A Social History*. Chapel Hill: University of North Carolina Press, 1937.

Mackay-Smith, Alexander. *The Colonial Quarter Race Horse*. Middleburg, Virginia: H. K. Groves, 1983.

Mann, Glenn E. (Ted). *A Story of Glory: Duke University Football*. Greenville, South Carolina: Doorway Publishers, 1985.

Morris, Ron. *ACC Basketball: An Illustrated History*. Chapel Hill: Four Corners Press, 1988.

Mumau, Thad. *The Dean Smith Story: More Than a Coach*. Huntsville, Alabama: Strode Publishers, 1980.

_____. *Go Wolfpack! North Carolina State Football*. Huntsville, Alabama: Strode Publishers, 1981.

News and Observer (Raleigh). *North Carolina Quadricentennial Edition*. Raleigh: News and Observer Publishing Company, 1985.

Rappoport, Ken. *Tar Heel: North Carolina Basketball*. Huntsville, Alabama: Strode Publishers, 1976.

_____. *Tar Heel: North Carolina Football*. Huntsville, Alabama: Strode Publishers, 1976.

Tufts, Richard S. *The Scottish Invasion, Being a Brief Review of American Golf in Relation to Pinehurst and the Sixty-second National Amateur*. Pinehurst: Pinehurst Publishers, 1962.

Watson, Alan D. *Society in Colonial North Carolina*. Raleigh: North Carolina Department of Cultural Resources, Division of Archives and History, 1975.

Wilkinson, Sylvia. *Dirt Tracks to Glory: The Early Days of Stock Car Racing as Told by Participants*. Chapel Hill: Algonquin Books, 1983.

ARTICLES

Beezley, William H. "The 1961 Scandal at North Carolina State and the End of the Dixie Classic," in Donald Chu, Jeffrey O. Seagrave, and Beverly J. Becker (eds.), *Sport and Higher Education*. Champaign, Illinois: Human Kinetics Publishers, Inc., 1985.

Gorn, Elliott J. "Gouge and Bite, Pull Hair and Scratch: The Social Significance of Fighting in the Southern Backcountry." *American Historical Review*, 90 (February, 1985).

Hatcher, P. Graham, and Charles A. Lewis. "The Evolution of Leisure Pursuits in the Lower Cape Fear Region, 1731-1860." *Lower Cape Fear Historical Society Journal*, XXXI (June, 1989).

Lemmon, Sarah McCulloh. "Entertainment in Raleigh in 1890." *North Carolina Historical Review*, XL (June, 1963).

Lewis, Henry W. "Horses and Horsemen in Northampton before 1900." *North Carolina Historical Review*, LI (April, 1974).

Lumpkin, Angela. "The Leisure Pursuits of North Carolina Upper-Class Women in the Twentieth Century." Unpublished paper presented at the fourteenth annual conference of the North American Society for Sport History, May 26, 1986. (Abstract published in *Proceedings of the Fourteenth NASSH Conference*, North American Society for Sport History, 1986.)

Parramore, Tom. "Gouging in Early North Carolina." *North Carolina Folklore Journal*, XXII (May, 1974).

Roberts, B. W. C. "Cockfighting: An Early Entertainment in North Carolina." *North Carolina Historical Review*, XLII (July, 1965).

Smith, Leverett. "Minor League Baseball in Rocky Mount." *Baseball Research Journal*, 7 (1978).

Stone, Richard. "The Graham Plan of 1935: An Aborted Crusade to De-emphasize College Athletics." *North Carolina Historical Review*, LXIV (July, 1987).

Sumner, Jim L. "Baseball at Salisbury Prison Camp." *Baseball History,* premier annual edition (1989).

_____. "The North Carolina Inter-Collegiate Foot-ball Association: The Beginnings of College Football in North Carolina." *North Carolina Historical Review*, LXV (July, 1988).

_____. "The North Carolina State Professional Baseball League of 1902." *North Carolina Historical Review*, LXIV (July, 1987).

_____. "The State Fair and the Development of Modern Sports in Late Nineteenth-Century North Carolina." *Journal of Sport History*, 15 (Summer, 1988).

_____. "William G. Bramham: The Czar of Minor League Baseball." *Carolina Comments*, XXXVII (July, 1989).

INDEX

"Barn Field" (Asheville), 26
Barnes, Billy, 71
Barnes, James, 4
Baseball: at Duke University, 67; at North Carolina A & M College, 29, 39; at North Carolina A & T State University, 39; at North Carolina State University, 67; at UNC-Chapel Hill, 39, 67; in early twentieth century, 36-39; in twentieth century, 45-48, 60-67; origins of, in antebellum period, 18; rise of, 24, 25-29
Basketball: at Appalachian State University, 86; at Campbell University, 86; at Davidson College, 80-81, 86; at Duke University, 76-77, 78-79, 80, 84-85; at East Carolina University, 86; at Guilford College, 86; at North Carolina A & T State University, 86; at North Carolina State University, 74-76, 77, 83-84; at UNC-Asheville, 86; at UNC-Chapel Hill, 74, 76, 77-78, 79-80, 82-83; at UNC-Charlotte, 85-86; at UNC-Wilmington, 86; at Wake Forest University, 76, 85; at Western Carolina University, 81, 86; at Winston-Salem State University, 81; professional, 88-89, 103
Batchelor, W. P., 25
Beasley, Genia, 89
Beatty, Jim, 93-94
Beck, Chip, 91
Bell, Peggy Kirk, 92
Bellamy, Walt, 80, 88
Bennett, Ben, 70
Benoit, Joan, 95
Benton, Horace, 61
Benton, Rube, 38
Berra, Yogi, 46
Berry, Jean, 69
Bershak, Andy, 49
Bertram (racehorse), 13
Bibby, Jim, 66
Bicycling, 31, 33-34
Biddle, Charles: quoted, 2
Biddle Institute (Charlotte): baseball at, 39; football at, 30, 40-41. *See also* Johnson C. Smith University
Big Filly (racehorse), 4

Big Five, 51, 53
Big Four, 71, 72, 76, 80, 81, 82, 85
Big South Conference, 86
Bilas, Jay, 85
Billiards: in antebellum period, 18
Biltmore (Asheville), 32
Bi-State League (baseball), 46
Black, Larry, 94
Blacks: as participants in sports in North Carolina, 6, 20, 34, 47-48, 56, 59, 79-80
Blank (racehorse), 12
Blass, Steve, 63
Bloomer, Amelia, 34
Bloomsbury Park (Raleigh), 43
Blue Ridge League (baseball), 60
Bluebonnet Bowl, 69
Boetticher, Otto, 26
Boggs, Wade, 63
Bogle, Johnny, 52
Bogues, Tyrone (Mugsy), 85
Bolton, Catherine, 90
Bolton, Cliff, 46
Bonds, Bobby, 63
Boone, Dan, 46
Boros, Julius, 90
Boston (racehorse), 14
Bouton, Jim, 63
Bowling: 102; early forms of, in antebellum period, 18
Boxing, 45, 101
Bradley, Scott, 67
Bradsher, Arthur, 39
Bramham, William G., 37, 46
Brayboy, Jack, 52
Brennan, Pete, 76, 86
Brewer, Kidd, 51
Brickell, John: quoted, 3
Brinkley, William, 5
Broderick Cup, 96
Brown, Alton, 61
Brown, Gates, 62
Brown, Larry, 89
Brown, Mack, 69
Brown, Skip, 85
Brown, Ted, 70, 74
Browne family, 5
Bryan, Billy, 74
Bryan, John, 14
Bryant, Kelvin, 69
Bubas, Vic, 77, 79, 84

108

Buehler, Al, 94, 96
Bull Durham (movie), 61
Bulla, Johnny, 55
Burgess, Smokey, 63
Burleson, Tommy, 83, 84
Butler, Brett, 63
Butler, John, 17
Bynum, Wade, 14
Byrd, Dennis, 70

C

Caldwell, Mike, 66, 67
Calhoun, Lee, 93
Calvin, Mack, 89
Cameron, Bennehan, 25
Cameron, Eddie, 51, 53
Cameron Indoor Stadium (Duke University), 53
Campbell University: basketball at, 86
"Cardiac Pack" (North Carolina State University basketball team, 1982-1983), 84
Carew, Rod, 63
Carnevale, Ben, 74
Carney, Stephen, 11, 12
Carolina Association (baseball league), 37
Carolina Cougars (of American Basketball Association), 89
Carolina Country Club (Raleigh), 54
Carolina 500 (stock-car race), 101
Carolina League (baseball), 60, 61, 62
Carolina Lightning (Charlotte), of American Soccer League, 103
Carolina Sports by Land and Water, 20
Carolinas Conference, 54
Carr, Kenny, 84, 88
Carr, M. L., 86
Carson family, 14
Carter/Carter-Finley Stadium (Raleigh), 70
Cartwright, Alexander, 26
Case, Everett, 74-76, 77, 78, 89
Casey, Willis, 98
Casper, Billy, 90
Castianira (racehorse), 11
Castor, Chris, 70
Catawba College: basketball at, 54; football at, 51

Central Intercollegiate Athletic Association (CIAA), 52, 81
Chaffin, William, 18-19
Chamberlain, Wilt, 76
Chambers family, 5
Chappell, Len, 78-79
Charles, Lorenzo, 84
Charleston (South Carolina) Jockey Club, 6
Charlotte Checkers (of Eastern Hockey League), 103
Charlotte Clippers (football team), 52
Charlotte Country Club, 42
Charlotte Hornets (of National Basketball Association), 103
Charlotte Hornets (of World Football League), 103
Charlotte Motor Speedway, 101
Charlotte Observer Marathon, 102
Charlotte Open (golf tournament), 90
Charlotte Speedway, 57
Chesley, Castleman D., 77
Christy, Dick, 70
Chungke (game played by native Americans), 6
Church, W. S., 25
Cincinnati Red Stockings (baseball team), 27
Claiborne, C. B., 80
Clark, Rusty, 79
Cloninger, Tony, 66
Coastal Plains League (baseball), 46, 60
Cockfighting: in antebellum period, 8-9, 15-16, 18; in colonial period, 2, 5; in early twentieth century, 42; in post-Civil War period, 23, 25
Cole, J. R., quoted, 18
Collins, Chuck, 49
Colonial Conference, 86
"Colored State Fair" (Raleigh), 34
Cook, Doug, 81
Corbett, Don, 86
Cotton Bowl, 67
Covington, Wes, 66
Craig, Roger, 66
Craven, Braxton, 18
Craven County Jockey Club, 14
Crawford, Fred, 50, 51
Crawford family, 5
Cremins, Bobby, 82, 86
Crockett family, 62

Crowder, Alvin, 47
Crowder, Zeb: quoted, 21
Crowell, John Franklin, 29, 30
Crozier, Richard, 41
Crum, Dick, 69
Crumpler, Carlester, 71
Culler, Richard Broadus, 54
Cunningham, Billy, 79, 88, 89
Currituck Shooting Club, 32
Curtis, Mike, 73
Cy Young Award, 63, 66

D

Daniel, Beverly, 14
Daugherty, Brad, 82
Davidson College: athletics at, 32; basketball at, 41, 54, 80-81, 86; football at, 30, 40, 51
Davie, Allen, 12-13
Davie, William R., 12
Davis, Charlie, 80
Davis, Lee, 81
Davis, Walter, 82, 88
Dawkins, Johnny, 85, 88
Dawson, John, 11
DeHart, James, 50
Dempsey, Jack, 45
DeRogatis, Al, 72
Dickey, Dick, 75
Dillon, John (Hook), 74
Dilweg, Anthony, 70
Diomed (racehorse), 11, 12
Dixie Classic (basketball tournament), 76, 78
Dixie League (football), 52
Donnelly, Rick, 69
Dooley, Bill, 68-69, 71
Drew, John (Halifax County owner of racehorses), 11
Drew, John (professional basketball player), 88
Driesell, Charles (Lefty), 80-81, 82, 86
Dubois, Peter: quoted, 7
Duke Indoor Stadium (Durham), 53
Duke Stadium (Durham), 50
Duke University: baseball at, 67; basketball at, 53, 76, 77, 78-79, 80, 84-85; football at, 49-51, 69-70; hosts international track and field meets, 96; soccer program at, 97; tennis at, 93; women's basketball at, 90;

women's golf at, 92. *See also* Trinity College
Duncan, Lawson, 93
Dunn, Karen, 96
Dupont, Laura, 93
Durham Bulls (baseball team), 61
Dye, Pat, 71

E

Earnhardt, Dale, 101
East Carolina Teachers College/University: baseball at, 67; basketball at, 86; football at, 71-72; sports program at, 56; women's basketball at, 90
Eastern Bowl, 71
Eastern Carolina Baseball League, 37
Eastern Carolina League (baseball), 46
Eaton, Thomas, 5
Edwards, Earle, 70
Elkins, Mike, 71
Elliot, William: quoted, 20
Ellis, Richard, 5
Elon College: basketball at, 41, 54; football at, 40, 51, 72
Emerson Field (UNC-Chapel Hill), 49
Emory, Ed, 72
Esposito, Sam, 67

F

Fairfield Jockey Club, 12
Feathers, Beattie, 70
Ferrell, George, 47
Ferrell, Rick, 47
Ferrell, Wes, 47, 61
Ferry, Danny, 85
Fetzer, Bill, 49
Fetzer, Bob, 49, 56
Few, William Preston, 49-50
Ficklen Stadium (East Carolina University), 71
Final Four, 76, 79, 80, 83, 84, 85
Fisher, Brian, 63
Fisher Park (Greensboro), 43
Fishing: by slaves, 21; in antebellum period, 8, 19, 20; in colonial period, 2, 6; in twentieth century, 57
Fives, 18
Flood, Curt, 62
Floyd, Raymond, 91
Floyd family, 5
Flur, Marc, 93

Foot racing (colonial period), 6, 18
Football: at Appalachian State University, 72; at Davidson College, 51; at Duke University, 49-50, 69-70; at East Carolina University, 71-72; at Elon College, 72; at Lenoir Rhyne College, 72; at North Carolina A & T State University, 72; at North Carolina Central University, 52, 72; at North Carolina State University, 51, 70-71; at Trinity College, 49, 50; at UNC-Chapel Hill, 29, 30, 49, 67-69; at Wake Forest University, 51, 71; at Western Carolina University, 72; early forms of, in antebellum period, 18; in early twentieth century, 39-41; in twentieth century, 45, 48-52; professional, 72-74; rise of, 29-31
Ford, Phil, 82, 88
Foster, Bill, 84, 85
Franklin, John Hope: quoted, 22
Free, Lloyd (World), 86, 88
Fulton, John, 14
Futch, Eunies, 89

G

Gabriel, Roman, 70, 73
Gaines, Clarence (Bighouse), 81, 86
Gallant Fox (racehorse), 13
Gambling: among native Americans, 6; in colonial period, 2
Gammon, Von, 31
Gander pulling, 17-18
Gantt, Bob, 39
Garber, Gene, 62
Garrity, Hank, 51
Gator Bowl, 68, 70, 71
Geiger, Betty Springs, 95
George, Bill, 72
Gibson, Josh, 47
Gibson, Mel, 81
Givens, Jack, 85
Glamack, George, 53, 87
Glenn, Alston, 94
Gminski, Mike, 84, 85, 88
Golf: beginnings of, 18, 32; in early twentieth century, 41, 42-43; in twentieth century, 45, 54-55, 90-92
Goodhall, Ellison, 96

Goodman, Billy, 63
Gorn, Elliot: quoted, 16
"Gouging": in antebellum period, 8, 9, 16-17, 18; in colonial period, 5, 6
Gould family, 5
Grace, Mark, 66
Graham, Frank Porter, 49
"Graham Plan," 49
Grand National Division (NASCAR), 99
Grange, Red, 45
Grant, Bitsy, 56
Gray, Charles Carroll: quoted, 26
Greason, Murray, 53
Great Raleigh Road Race, 102
Greater Greensboro Open (golf tournament), 54, 90
Green, Kenny, 85
Greenberg, Hank, 46
Greenlee, Marion, 48
Greensboro Country Club, 42
Griffin, Rod, 85
Grimm, Charles, 46
Groat, Dick, 67, 76, 86-87
Grubar, Dick, 79
Gudger, Jim, 81
Guilford College: basketball at, 41, 54, 86; football at, 30, 40, 51
Gymnastics: beginnings of, 31; on college campuses in early twentieth century, 41

H

Haas, Jay, 92
Haddix, Harvey, 61
Haddock, Jesse, 92
Hagen, Walter, 45
Hairston, Happy, 80
Hall, Jimmie, 66
Hallberg, Gary, 92
Hamilton, John, 11
Hanburger, Chris, 68, 73
Hanes Hosiery (Winston-Salem), 89
Harden, George, 25
Harp, Tom, 69
Hart, Jim Ray, 66
Harvey, Bill, 91
Heafner, Clayton, 55, 91
Heafner, Vance, 91
Hebner, Richie, 62
Heinrichs, April, 98-99

Meadows, Ed, 69, 72
Means, George, 25
Mebane Hunting Lodge (Rockingham County), 32
Meredith College: intramural sports at, 56
Methodist College: basketball at, 86
Middle Atlantic Tournament (tennis, Charlotte), 55
Mid-East Athletic Conference (MEAC), 81, 86
Miller, Larry, 79, 89
Miller, "Pud," 61
Mize, Johnny, 46
Mock, Bill, 53
Mock, C. D., 98
Moe, Doug, 89
Molodet, Vic, 75
Monkey (racehorse), 4
Monkey Island Club, 32
Monroe, Earl (The Pearl), 81, 88
Moonlight Race (Maggie, North Carolina), 102
Moorman, Tee, 69
Moreland, Chris, 90
Moreland, Jackie, 77, 78
Morey, Dale, 91
Morgan, Joe, 63
Morse, Jedediah, 16
Mowfield (Northampton County), 13
Mud Colt (racehorse), 4
Mullins, Jeff, 79, 86, 88
Murcer, Bobby, 63
Murphy, James, 14
Murray, Bill, 69
Murray, Eddie, 63
Myers, Elmer, 37
Myers Park Country Club (Charlotte), 54

N

Naismith, James, 41
Narrows Island Club, 32
Nash, Abner, 5
National Association for Stock Car Auto Racing (NASCAR), 99-101
National Association of Base Ball Players, 26
National Association of Intercollegiate Athletics (NAIA), 54, 81, 86

National Association of Professional Baseball Leagues, 36, 37, 46
National Basketball Association (NBA), 86-88
National Collegiate Athletic Association (NCAA): basketball tournaments, 53, 74, 76, 78, 79-80, 81, 82, 83, 84, 85, 86
National 500 (stock-car race), 101
National Football League (NFL), 52
National Invitational Tournament (NIT), 82, 84, 85
National League (baseball), 27, 36
Native Americans: as participants in sports in North Carolina, 6
Native Dancer (racehorse), 13
Natural History of North Carolina: quoted, 3
Negro Leagues, 47-48, 60
Nelson, Byron, 54
Nelson, Larry, 90
Nesbit, Joan, 96
Nettles, Graig, 63
New York Knickerbockers (baseball club), 26
Newman, Ed, 74
Nixon, Otis, 66
North and South Amateur Tournament (golf), 43
North and South Championship (tennis tournament), 55
North and South Women's Amateur (golf tournament), 43
North Carolina A & M Athletic Association, 31
North Carolina A & M College: baseball at, 29, 39; basketball at, 41; football at, 30, 40. *See also* North Carolina State University
North Carolina A & T State University: baseball at, 39; basketball at, 54, 86; football at, 40-41, 51-52, 72
North Carolina Central University: football at, 52, 72
North Carolina College. *See* North Carolina Central University
North Carolina Industrial Association, 34
North Carolina Intercollegiate Football Association, 30

Ray, Carl, 37
Reality (racehorse), 13
Red Cubans (breed of fighting birds), 25
Red Wasp (racehorse), 14
Reed, Tom, 70-71
Reid, J. R., 82
Rein, Bo, 70
Reiss, Matt, 98
Rennie, John, 97
Rerych, Steve, 98
Reynolds, Ellen, 96
Reynolds Coliseum (North Carolina State University), 75
Rhodes, Ike, 25
Richards, Vincent, 55
Richter, Jim, 70, 74
Riddick Field (North Carolina State University), 70
Righetti, Dave, 63
Ripken, Cal, 63
Rippay, Benjamin. See Jones, Charles Wesley
Rizzuto, Phil, 46
Robert Burns (racehorse). See Sir Archie
Roche, John, 80
Rockne, Knute, 45
Rodriguez, Chi Chi, 90
Roosevelt, Theodore, 39-40
Roper, Jim, 99
Rose, Clarence, 91
Rose Bowl, 50, 51
Rosen, Al, 61
Rosenbluth, Lennie, 76, 86
Ross, Donald, 43
Rounders, 18
Rugby, 31
Rupp, Adolph, 74-75
Ruth, Babe, 38, 45, 47

S
Sadri, John, 93
St. Augustine's College: baseball at, 39; basketball at, 86
Salisbury Jockey Club, 10-11, 14
Sampson, Ralph, 84
Sand Hill School (Buncombe County), 26
Sanders, Doug, 90
Sanford, Terry, 78
Sanguillen, Manny, 62
Santa Ana (president of Mexico), 16
Schaw, Janet: quoted, 6
Scott, Charlie, 79-80, 88
Scott, George, 63
Seabrooks, Kelvin, 101
Sedgefield Country Club (Guilford County), 55
Seixas, Vic, 93
Sermon, Doc, 53
Severin, Paul, 49
Shaffer, Lee, 88
Shankle, Joel, 93
Shavlik, Ronnie, 75, 86
Shaw University: baseball at, 39; football at, 40-41
Shea, Julie, 95, 96
Shea, Mary, 95
Shepard, Norman, 54
Sheridan, Dick, 71
Shinny. See bandy
Shoals, Leo (Muscle), 61
Shocco Game Association (Warren County), 32
Shooting matches (in antebellum period), 18
Shore, Ernie, 38
Shute, Denny, 54
Sifford, Charlie, 91
Sime, Dave, 93
Simmons, Floyd (Chunk), 93
Sindelar, Joey, 90
Sir Archie (racehorse), 11-14, 21
Sir Charles (racehorse), 13, 14
Skakle, Don, 93
Ski Beech, 102
Skiing, 102
Slaughter, Enos (Country), 63
Slaves: participate in sports in colonial and antebellum periods, 6, 20, 21; uses of, in connection with horse racing, 21
Sloan, Norm, 83, 84
Sloan, Steve, 69
Smawley, Belus, 87
Smith, Al, 55
Smith, Carr, 46
Smith, Dean, 79, 82-83
Smith, J. D., 73
Smith, James (Bonecrusher), 101

Smith, John: quoted, 21
Smith, Kenny, 82
Smith, Lloyd, 46
Smith Center (UNC-Chapel Hill), 83
Smyth, J. F. D.: quoted, 3
Snavely, Carl, 49, 67-68
Snead, Norm, 71, 73
Snead, Sam, 54, 90
Snyder, Dick, 81
Soccer: 97; origins of, in antebellum period, 18
Softball, 102
Souchak, Mike, 90, 91
South Atlantic League (baseball), 46, 61, 62
Southern Conference, 45, 49, 53, 54, 69, 71, 72, 75, 76, 81, 86
Southern Intercollegiate Athletic Association, 29
Southern League (baseball), 28, 46, 61-62
Southern League (football), 52
Southern Pines: holds "Week of Sport," 33
Southerners: Portrait of a People: quoted, 45
Spanarkel, Jim, 84, 85
Speight, Bobby, 75
Spinks, Leon, 101
Spinks, Michael, 101
Spirit of the Times, 11
Springs, Betty. *See* Geiger, Betty Springs
Spurrier, Steve, 69
Staak, Bob, 85
Stargell, Willie, 63
Starmount Forest Country Club (Greensboro), 54
Stasavich, Clarence, 71, 72
State Fair. *See* North Carolina State Fair
State Game Commission, 57, 102
State Jockey Club, 14
Statesville Athletic Club, 41
Staub, Rusty, 63
Steele, John, 14
Stewart, Flucie, 51
Stock-car racing, 99-101
Stoddard, Tim, 67
Stottlemyre, Mel, 63

Strange, Curtis, 92
Stranger in America, The (1807), 16
Strother, David Hunter: quoted, 16
Stubbs, Franklin, 66
Sugar Bowl, 51, 67
Sugar Mountain, 102
Suggs, George, 38
Sullivan Award, 94
Summerell, Carl, 71
Surhoff, B. J., 67
Swan Island Club, 32
Swindell, J. E., 37

T

Tacy, Carl, 85
Tangerine Bowl, 71
Tanglewood (Forsyth County), 54
Tar Heel League (baseball), 60
Tatum, Jim, 68
Tayloe, John, III, 12
Taylor, Arthur, 12
Taylor, Bernard, 101
Taylor, Charles, 48
Taylor, Lawrence, 69, 73-74, 102
Taylor, Scott, 98
Taylor family, 5
"Team of a Million Backs, The", 49
Tebell, Gus, 51, 53
Temple, Johnny, 63
Tenace, Gene, 63
Tennis: at UNC-CH, 56; beginnings of, 31, 32; in early twentieth century, 41, 42, 43; in twentieth century, 45, 55-56
Thacker, Tab, 98
Thomas, Herb, 101
Thompson, David, 83, 84, 88, 94
Thompson, Speedy, 101
Thorpe, Jim (native American athlete of Pennsylvania), 37
Thorpe, Jim (professional golfer of Roxboro), 91
Tilden, Bill, 45, 55
Timoleon (racehorse), 13, 14
Tipton, Eric, 50, 51
Tobacco State League (baseball), 60
Tolley, Jerry, 72
Tompkins, Daniel A., 30-31
Tovar, Cesar, 62
Towe, Monte, 83
Townball, 25. *See also* rounders

White, Roy, 63
Whitehead, Burgess, 47
Whitney, Charles (Hawkeye), 84
Whitted, George (Possum), 38
Whittenberg, Derek, 84
Whittle, Heath, 56
Wilhelm, Hoyt, 61, 63, 66
Wilkerson, Doug, 73
Wilkinson, Jay, 69
Wilkinson, Tim, 93
Willard, Ken, 68, 73
Williamson, Harry, 56
Wilmington Committee of Safety: quoted, 7
Wilmington Jockey Club, 6, 7, 10
Wilson, Red, 69, 72
Winston-Salem State College/University: basketball at, 81, 86
Wolf, Joe, 82
Wolf, Ray, 49
Women: as participants in sports, 22, 33, 56, 59-60, 89
Wood, Al, 82
Wood, Wilbur, 63
Wooten, Ron, 69
World Golf Hall of Fame (Pinehurst), 91

World Open (golf tournament), 91
World 600 (stock-car race), 101
Wormeley, Ralph, 12
Worthy, James, 82, 88
Wrangler (racehorse), 12
Wrestling: at North Carolina State University, 98; at UNC-Chapel Hill, 98; in colonial period, 6, 18
Wright, Taffy, 47
Wuycik, Dennis, 82

Y

YMCA, 41, 43, 53
YWCA, 43, 89
Yarborough, Cale, 101
Yastrzemski, Carl, 62
Young, Auguston, 94
Young, Danny, 85
Younger, Monk, 51, 54
Yount, Floyd, 61
Yow, Kay, 89-90
Yow, Virgil, 54, 89

Z

Zachary, Tom, 47
Zernial, Gus, 61
Zisk, Richie, 63

About the Author

Jim L. Sumner, a native of Fort Bragg, North Carolina, was reared in nearby Saint Pauls. He holds a B.A. in history from Duke University and an M.A. in history from North Carolina State University and is presently employed as a historian for the State Historic Preservation Office of the North Carolina Division of Archives and History. Sumner is the author of numerous scholarly and popular articles on sports history, particularly in the realm of baseball. In addition, he has served as coauthor of *Architectural Resources of Downtown Asheville* (1979) and contributed to the *Quadricentennial History of North Carolina*, published by the Raleigh *News and Observer* in 1984, as well as to the forthcoming *Encyclopedia of the American Revolution*.

mids